THE SPIRITUAL SIGNIFICANCE
OF OVERLOAD BOREDOM

The Spiritual Significance of Overload Boredom

SHARDAY C. MOSURINJOHN

McGill-Queen's University Press
Montreal & Kingston • London • Chicago

ISBN 978-0-2280-1152-1 (cloth)
ISBN 978-0-2280-1153-8 (paper)
ISBN 978-0-2280-1329-7 (ePDF)
ISBN 978-0-2280-1330-3 (ePUB)

Legal deposit third quarter 2022
Bibliothèque nationale du Québec

Printed in Canada on acid-free paper that is 100% ancient forest free (100% post-consumer recycled), processed chlorine free

Funded by the Government of Canada | Financé par le gouvernement du Canada | Canada | Canada Council for the Arts | Conseil des arts du Canada

We acknowledge the support of the Canada Council for the Arts.

Nous remercions le Conseil des arts du Canada de son soutien.

Library and Archives Canada Cataloguing in Publication

Title: The spiritual significance of overload boredom / Sharday C. Mosurinjohn.

Names: Mosurinjohn, Sharday C., author.

Description: Includes bibliographical references and index.

Identifiers: Canadiana (print) 20220175632 | Canadiana (ebook) 20220175721 | ISBN 9780228011521 (cloth) | ISBN 9780228011538 (paper) | ISBN 9780228013297 (ePDF) | ISBN 9780228013303 (ePUB)

Subjects: LCSH: Boredom. | LCSH: Aesthetics. | LCSH: Arts. | LCSH: Meaning (Philosophy) | LCSH: Caring—Moral and ethical aspects. | LCSH: Technology—Psychological aspects.

Classification: LCC BF575.B67 M67 2022 | DDC 152.4—dc23

This book was typeset by Marquis Interscript in 10.5/13 Sabon.

To TGW; yes.

Contents

Figures

Preface

I care about boredom. I find it meaningful. It has helped me make sense of experiences of meaninglessness. Since experience does not come separable along pre-perforated lines, our concepts act like scissors and boredom cuts a particular shape that fits a vital set of questions about time and existential meaning. I have found that boredom puts us face to face with our being in time, the nature of our interiority, what does and does not matter to us, and what sources of legitimacy we have appealed to in order to guarantee that mattering, or meaning. This is why, and, depending on the idiom, boredom is a matter of "spiritual" significance.[1]

I am here to tell you we are not bored the way we used to be: boredom has changed and we barely noticed. This matters. And it can and will be read as a spiritual crisis. Boredom has always articulated a suite of existential concerns involving human subjectivity and temporality, but now those concerns are being transformed in relation to information and technology. These transformations exert new pressures on us in the present; atmospheric and overloading. Here is how I came to perceive this shift, and what it means for us.

* * *

I have always been haunted by the fundamental arbitrariness of my every action. According to the world I grew up with, which I would describe as secular and materialist, nothing meant anything unless I chose to give it personal meaning. I was not raised in any cultural, familial, religious, or other tradition that was ever named as such. The closest I come to a nameable tradition was through my mother, a "recovering" Irish Catholic. So Irish Catholic was what I was "not," and therefore cast a shadow over whatever I "was." We would ask St Anthony for help whenever we lost, say, an earring, or a key. The "punching nun" toy we sometimes topped our Christmas tree with was a visual gag whose underlying grievance was the corporal punishment my mother ultimately ran away from at the Catholic school of her childhood. The worldview of a particular tradition could be glimpsed, but the possibility of participation in anything like a community was far out of sight.

I understood, as I matured, that although I felt orphaned by tradition, I was by no means living a value-neutral social existence. I had the standard-issue liberal values of hegemonic Christian Canadian society and the scientific materialist framework of my formal education. Yet, neither helped me reconcile my desire to appeal to something beyond personal choice for existential meaning. In terms of worldview, I saw no plausible alternatives, so personal choice described the ambit of meaning in my world.

I began, therefore, to think that the issue I had might be with choice itself. The day-to-day kinds of choices that made up my life path – career, hobbies, relationships, aspirations, lifestyle, etc. I was tyrannized by choice. And the tyranny of choice was amplified by the recognition that the privilege to choose came with an imperative to choose correctly … according to? I did not know. I thus came to realize that it was not just the choices, it was also the choosing; there were implausibly many different heuristics to choose from in order to decide how to make the choice. An infinite regress of choice.

The logical extension of this thinking was to question: where do all these choices come from? It seemed to me that they were the result of being exposed to information, whether with respect to consumer goods or worldviews, actions or sensations, ideas or images. So much information, so fast, that you cannot forget enough of it to make space for thorough consideration, and therefore, for making careful distinctions between a meaningful or a meaningless choice.

Making this link between choice and information then revealed another dimension that would become important to my project: time and temporality. Whereas "choice" conjured for me the notion of a decision point – an "either/or" branching of a timeline – "information" conjured the thought of something moving through time, a matter of speed, effusion, limited only by physical constants and the media conveying it. I reframed my intuition about the problem of arbitrariness in relation to the vastness of information. Particularly, the information I would never have enough time to process, and the fact that the limited amount of that total information that I *was* taking in was still too much, even though my life was dedicated to thinking, reading, and writing.

The volume and speed of information was overwhelming to the temporality of my mind|body.[2] I wondered if, to everyone else, this was so massive, and therefore so obvious and so *intractable* a problem that they did not bother to give it much attention. I, however, found it urgent, because I experienced it as the fracturing of the timeline of my life and any coherent narrative it might tell, and as the over-extension of my capacity to sense, and attend, and care. Catalyzed by this temporal and affective crisis, I began studying time in philosophy and art.[3] It was through both channels that I came upon boredom as a concept that linked together all of my concerns. In boredom, my philosophy and my art found their frame.[4]

In phenomenological philosophy, boredom was often characterized as a warping of time – specifically, a slowing, stilling, or emptying of time. This state of emptied time tends to compel certain questions: why is time stuck? what *is* time? how should I pass it? Seeing time unfurnished and stretching out to the edges of human reckoning the profoundly bored might ask: why, ultimately, should I make this choice? why that one? why anything? In fact, why is there something rather than nothing? This is why boredom can be an existentially attuning sort of state.

In the art world, boredom appeared often as a concern of the mid-twentieth-century conceptualists and those who followed. Within their work, I paid attention to temporal experimentation with how long the artist or the audience could endure boring conditions like silence or repetition. The nature of the repetition was often determined by enabling constraints stipulated by the artist, as in "instruction pieces," where artists would write instructions that others would execute. These were essentially algorithms for generating and corralling information, which resonated loudly with my own interest in dealing with information overload.[5]

My thinking about boredom consolidated as I moved to focus upon the distinction between contemporary boredom and its earlier forms. This distinction is illuminated by the way certain twenty-first-century artworks explore boredom and information technology – specifically, artworks that sustain a critical reflection on the temporality of everyday life through information. All of the art objects I write about in this book contend with the temporality of information overload by aestheticizing[6] what is too vast and too fast to be perceived.

My initial framing of this project was that boredom had transformed in the face of information- and choice overload to become a distinctive form of late modern temporality.[7] However, over the years, the result of my various enquiries into phenomenology, information theory, and even trends in the new materialisms was the theorizing of my concept "overload boredom."[8] This, I define primarily in affective terms instead of temporal ones. When I write of overload boredom, I am not just writing about the psychological emotion of boredom, nor of boredom as a *lack* of emotion; I think of overload boredom as a *dis*affect. I associate the *disaffect* of overload boredom with its relatives of anxiety, loneliness, melancholy, and other psychic pains related to the collective transformations of choice, information, and time that I have just described. Overload both creates more object encounters and dampens our ability to sense withdrawal and the resultant loneliness and melancholy; it is in this way that overload boredom disaffects.

Overload boredom therefore names both a withdrawal from the bombardments of ubiquitous info-tech, and also the impossibility of properly withdrawing into a human interiority colonized by the same.[9] Overload boredom makes its own workings *imperceptible*: it hides the fact that it is hidden. To uncover it, I have decided here to speculate aesthetically. To look at how art objects make sensible the imperceptibility of overload boredom.

* * *

Stepping back and taking a broad view of my work to this point, I cannot help but think about what conceptual artist Douglas Huebler once said: "the world is full of objects, more or less interesting, I do not wish to add any more" (in Stiles and Selz 1996, 840). If I am going to be part of the information overload problem by writing a book, as expected in my field, then at least I can be part of the solution at the same time. This is my curatorial impulse: to synthesize a massive problem into a two-word paradigm of overload boredom, and to sustain focused thinking/feeling about it through a careful selection of artworks. Because of our imbrication in networked cognitive assemblages there is no way out of the oversaturated media ecology. I hope to show you that better relations with this ecology depend on attuning to overload boredom as a ubiquitous and inescapable dimension of contemporary life.

Acknowledgments

This project began under the mentorship of Gary Kibbins, and I am grateful for his guidance, his embrace of the weird and the metaphysical in theory and in art, and for his friendship. At that early stage, Michael Gardiner and Julian Jason Haladyn were generous with ideas, support, and opportunities. Their collegiality was pivotal to the trajectory of my research. Richard Ascough supported this work during my year as a postdoctoral fellow at Queen's School of Religion and since then as faculty member there. Over the years, Scott Lougheed has offered his insight on most of these chapters. My thinking and writing have benefited equally from his detailed feedback and from our wide-ranging conversations. Nelly Matorina brought her brilliance to the crossings between art and science required in the *For Boredom* website. Donovan Schaefer, Ryan Johnson, and Dustin Atlas originally made me feel welcome in circles where religion and affect were mixing. Their intellectual and material hospitality expanded my sense of the field. I was fortunate that Dustin later became my departmental colleague and friend, and continued to read revisions till the bitter end. All errors are his. I am grateful to my editor Khadija Coxon at McGill-Queen's University Press for letting me keep that joke in. I am lucky to have an editor with such tremendous skill, curiosity, creativity, and many other gifts besides. Erik Ewing-Meyer made contributions to a late draft of the manuscript. Jacob Boss and Jeremy Cohen, my co-founders at the Human Augmentation Research Network, have been incredible thought partners and a kind of intellectual home base. In my own home, my daughter Abiella grew up so much as I finished this book that she put the lie to one of my favourite comedy bits about boredom and parenthood – "I'm bored more than I love you."

Vincent Sacco has been an inexhaustible source of support, knowledge, and humour. Nathan Townend's confidence has inspired me tremendously. Many others have shaped my approach to scholarship along the way, and I am grateful to be in their company.

THE SPIRITUAL SIGNIFICANCE OF OVERLOAD BOREDOM

Introduction

The Spiritual Significance of Boredom

To be, in a word, unborable ... is the key to modern life. If you are immune to boredom, there is literally nothing you cannot accomplish.

David Foster Wallace, *The Pale King*

There is no immunity from a boredom born of overload. This boredom is a mode of existence that wants for meaning, but remains aspirational – an experience of *desiring* meaning, but struggling to perceive meaningful choices within the omnipresent and ephemeral cloud of information that is the atmosphere of data-driven, info-capitalist, late modern culture. This is a boredom that interrupts and unsettles thought, feeling, and physicality. It forces consciousness to turn in on itself but this interiority is no retreat from an atmosphere saturated with far too much of everything. The inside has been intruded upon by noise from the outside. Its affects are anesthetic: alienation, uncertainty, mystification. In this glossy haze, the self becomes estranged from itself. The only viable response seems to be a withdrawal from the info-sphere, each other, and our own entropic interiority. But that leaves nowhere to go, and no time left to get there. Time loses its phenomenology, experience empties its qualities.

But this boredom, as with all boredom, is paradoxical. As it undermines contemplation it also offers to renew insight. It riddles with questions of what might be meaningful and what meaning even *is*. This is a boredom that chases the void with questions about life, existence, and our place in it; it is a *spiritual* boredom. It is also a distinctly twenty-first century boredom. It is what I call "overload boredom" and it is different from the boredoms that have come before it and those that coexist with it.

Psychologically speaking, "boredom" refers to a mix of "emotions such as frustration, surfeit, depression, disgust, indifference, apathy, and that feeling of being trapped or confined" (Toohey 2011, 13).[1] This private psychological capacity for boredom affects the individual and may come and go without significantly altering the affects of the public world. Yet expressions of this psychological capacity are always shaped by the collective *technologies of sensation* as well as the relational configurations of humans and other beings.[2] While focus on individual, or psychological, boredom may well be of therapeutic benefit, this study will focus on the interplay between the isolated and the over-connected in order to understand the collective technologies, pathologies, and particularities of contemporary overload boredom.

Historically, "boredom" is a modern English-language concept that tracked the existential alienations of modernization: secularization, urbanization, bureaucratization, rationalization, technologization, and, above all, the democratization of existential doubt.[3] To make this last matter worse, it was *homo faber*'s own handiwork that procured this generalized alienation. Not merely labour, but scientific and speculative achievements, too, served to estrange the modern subject. From Kepler's *Optics* (1604), which proposed that the eye is separate from what it sees, to Galileo's telescope and onward, philosophy and science continued, tormentingly, to reveal that our senses could not be trusted, and some form of mediation was always wedged between the world and our experience of it (Arendt 1958; Haladyn 2015). Modern boredom was a form of self-conscious mediation in response to recognizing both the withdrawnness of the world and the onslaught of modern demands; it was "experience without qualities" (Goodstein 2005). Modern boredom was therefore a cultural affect, as it was linked to social fragmentation, experiencing the linear clock time of capitalist manufacture, and thinking about human existence in a world without known boundaries. Produced by historical and social contingencies, modern boredom affected the group level, colouring the feeling tone of the social world. It set the historical stage for overload boredom.

However, neither modern nor overload boredom replaces or fully determines the many versions of "simple" or fleeting bored feelings that one might feel while waiting in a waiting room with no cell signal or WiFi, or sitting through an unnecessary meeting. Each is layered on the other. Twenty-first century overload boredom inherits modern boredom, and transforms it through processes of informationalization, digitalization, virtualization, and acceleration.[4] This is how it can be that overload boredom is brimming with content, but empty of meaning. Noise and banality stymie interpretive ability. Failure to interpret relationships of difference, similarity, and pattern in the signs of life in the info-sphere means that their qualities do not manifest in our experience. Overload boredom surfaces as the problem of how to handle the blooming buzzing confusion of the raw materials of meaning.[5] These materials consist of information, the technology that provides it nonstop, and the cultural structures that pressure users to attach their sense of moral worth to making the correct choice.

CHOICE OVERLOAD

As the sociologist Peter Berger (1979) acknowledged, the awareness of alternatives to choose from and the requirement to make a choice weakens the meaning, value, and plausibility of all the choices available to us. He names this concept the "heretical imperative," a nod to the Greek word *haireîn* that is at the root of the general concept of choice and the religious concept of heresy. The heretical imperative helps us understand how choice, in a condition of information overload (e.g., Andrejevic 2013; Levitin 2014; Levitin 2015), becomes tyrannizing rather than liberating. That is, the possibility of choice appears to be a precondition of freedom, but the confrontation of endless choices – which must be faced, no less, without the benefit of shared heuristics provided by overarching metaphysical systems – is paralyzing. Everything feels heretical; opposed to the norms of some undefined system.

Making a choice requires us to draw upon some logic for evaluating alternatives, and many of these alternatives are mutually exclusive and also seemingly interchangeable. The infinite substitutability of personal choices is reinforced by the ways that a logic of substitutability dominates the world; in the abstract equivalence of money, in the "substitution of the circulation of things for human relations" (Legge 2016, 92), in the similarity of form taken by both labour and leisure as they are channelled through the same devices, in the way that pursuing a spectacular succession of novelties becomes, itself, repetitious, and all of which seems to drain "the world of qualitative differences" (Gardiner 2016, 243). My choices appear either as essentially interchangeable, and therefore might as well be random, or as without social consequence, and therefore pointless.

But if we agree that we are in any way responsible for our choices, then it nonetheless seems reasonable to increase our possibilities. For example, we may be able to work from home, or earn an online degree on our own schedule (examples that may resonate especially in the quarantine era of the novel coronavirus pandemic). This may seem like a kind of freedom, but we should notice how it "diffuses 'responsibility'" to make choices throughout life (Crain 2013). Here, choice slides between the individual register and an affective structure of suspension, disengagement, and ambivalence that sees us pursue the opening of choice wider and wider. We pursue this kind of opening up, but as the bandwidth of choice expands, it distorts the reference points of our shared meanings. Consequently, the logic of our choice-making becomes less systematic and more random, and, in turn, we become less able to recognize ourselves through the movement of our own will. And yet, it seems we cannot ethically stop this process of opening and choosing. As Carl Elliott observed, "once self-fulfillment is hitched to the success of a human life, it comes perilously close to an obligation" (2004, 303).

Choice is thus an unavoidable double agent of possibility and foreclosure, creating the illusion of infinite possibility while trapping us in moral failure. What happens is that the illusion of unlimited choice forces individuals to take responsibility for what is actually a *system failure*, all while appearing to grant them freedom (freedom they cannot reject [see, e.g., Kotsko 2018]). So, if an individual fails it appears to be because they made the wrong choice and therefore any resulting aggression, doubt, or anxiety belongs at least partly turned back on themselves (Salecl 2009). Individuals are left alone to bear responsibility for their own failings, *mystifying* their inextricability from collective life. This is because the illusion of unlimited choice under late modern logic has a way of masking its own workings.

In reality, choice is limited by more than individual shortcomings, but in theory there is no upper limit that could be placed on desire and demand for social, material, or whatever goods. This state of disconnect between limited agency and unlimited desire is characterized by a constant tension that has been variously called "overchoice" (Toffler 1970), "the paradox of choice" (Schwartz 2004), "the tyranny of choice" (Salecl 2011), and the phrase I favour, "choice overload" (Iyengar and Lepper 2000). Choice overload is the apotheosis of the heretical imperative. What is left in its wake is overload boredom.

That is, we are all overloaded by information. Sometimes we experience this as an overload of choice, especially when we do not have systems of curation to herd, corral, and organize the torrential flow of info, as we will see in chapter 6. Eroding a basic sense of voluntariness, its cumulative effect is one of disaffect, a self-protective withdrawal from the world, and a visceral rejection of the obligation of self-making. While choice overload is the consequence of the twenty-first century info-sphere, overload boredom is the disaffect that mediates its atmosphere.

FOUNDATIONS OF A THEORY OF OVERLOAD BOREDOM

The theory of overload boredom I am proposing can act like a compass, reorienting our relationships to information, information technologies, and cultural logics that make these things matter; more importantly, it is a social diagnostic meant to index a *collective* problem, more than a description of a psychological state. I identify an array of perceptions emerging from information and choice overload: warped temporality; withdrawal from interiority; and a suite of disaffects, including, of course, boredom. I collect these into a new concept: overload boredom. As overload boredom *appears* through individuals, there is a temptation to provide individual solutions. I suggest we resist this move. Overload boredom is an affective consequence of a collective problem, and can only be addressed through attention to this collective breakdown. To that end, I examine the logics of social institutions and their processes (info-capitalism), their key values (self-making), and their modes of practice and interaction (habitual[6] media use) which, by design or by happenstance, burden users with heavy loads of choice and information.[7]

The social institutions, processes, and interactions I am interested in are all structured by what Franco Berardi calls info-capitalism.[8] Info-capitalism is the latest incarnation of capitalism to dominate the globe. It is characterized by processes like the digitalization of communication, and the performance of cognitive and affective labour, which occur far outside of traditional market contexts. Info-capitalism does not work evenly across all cultures; the idea that it does is a fantasy that belongs to info-capitalism itself. I must be clear, then, that I am speaking about a particular culture's experience of boredom, using a Western canon. Assuming that boredom, time, and information work in generally the same way for all people is buying into info-capitalism's erasure of alternative experiences and negotiations of boredom, as well as boredom's relationship to spirituality. Nevertheless, it is fair to say that one of the hallmarks of late modern Western temporality is overload boredom.[9]

The dominant representation of time in the modern Western imaginary is the linear image of the "timeline" of successive events. The timeline is slashed through with the eternal present of the "now," calibrating an interminable looping through the clock time of production and consumption. As the philosopher Mark Kingwell (2019a) writes:

> The social costs of the attention economy have been documented: rise in menial jobs, like packaging Amazon products, which are then systematically phased out by automation, robotics, and drones; the dominance of short-term and service jobs that have no security and no infrastructure; the so far marginal but still significant costs of inactivity and the screen-dominated life. But the central costs are perhaps less obvious. Boredom is never just the property of imagination-poor teenagers or over-imaginative philosophers. When we ourselves become the product we consume, the notion of work has decisively shifted. In the past, work was recognized for its colonizing power, expanding to fill and dominate time itself such that there might exist no clear line between work hours and nonwork hours. Our current condition is worse. The Interface, leveraging boredom, makes us all into unpaid workers for the advertisers who support those apparently cost-free platforms. We ought to recall that there is no such thing as a free transaction. In this species of transaction, you pay with your individuality, freedom, and happiness.

The new info-capitalist economy, as it leverages boredom, strips us of those very things that our modern liberal cultural has trained us to pursue. This leveraging of boredom involves modulations of our temporality, becoming fast and slow. Fast is the speed at which volumes of info content circulate on account of the fact that the workers and the products are one in the same, and labouring constantly at fibre-optic speeds. Slow is the drag of that content being noisy, meaning-poor, and alienating us from ourselves. The particular cultural context under examination here is exactly this: we have become a new kind of worker cum commodity. The resulting injustice is that we not only suffer from boredom, but we are tasked with making ourselves bored, and then told our boredom lacks significance.

At some point, the info-sphere itself "adopts the tone of weary, bored insouciance" (Gardiner 2014, 43) like an inoculation that dulls us to the symptomatic prompts of boredom to change our lives, rather than merely make better spectacles of ourselves. Since this is the scale of my critique, I discuss overload boredom not through case studies of particular incidents of choice and information overload, but through certain "scenarios"; namely, texting, social media presencing, and information work.[10] I find each of these scenarios in a twenty-first century art object that deals with boredom and information overload: I deal with texting through the poem *W8ING* by Sophia Le Fraga (2014); social media presencing through the poem *i feel better after i type to you* by Thomas Claburn and AOL user 23187425 (2006); and aesthetic attempts at dealing with vast amounts of information through the novel *The Pale King* by David Foster Wallace (2011).

What I like about exploring these scenarios through art objects is that they highlight information's materiality. They body forth information in its social role in institutional processes, in its affective role in in-forming bodies, and in the form of art objects. These scenarios give me the space to analyze in a mode inspired by the philosophy of "everyday aesthetics,"[11] which means looking at the everyday information practices thematized within the art objects in the same way I analyze the art objects themselves. I also draw on critical theories of late modernity, affect theory, and speculative realism. These theories help me capture the interplay of sensation, emotion, and cognition at play in overload scenarios. Methodologically and theoretically, I am aiming at a theorization of information as it relates to overload conditions, and the disaffect of overload boredom. Analytically, I recast boredom's hallmark features – its warped temporality and the way it forestalls the setting of even temporary, provisionally satisfying ends – in terms germane to the twenty-first century. That is, in terms that highlight the relevancy of considering boredom as a *spiritual crisis*.

SPIRITUAL CRISIS

My use of the adjective "spiritual" above comes from an emic boredom context of modern Europe where, for artists of the day, boredom was a "synecdoche for the spiritual crisis" of modernity (Goodstein 2005, 224). Though it is not bound by them, my theory of overload boredom does include some conceptions of boredom that appear in formally religious circumstances (e.g., Raposa 1999). However, in *The Spiritual Significance of Overload Boredom* I am not interested in smuggling an unarticulated theory of religion. I view forms of contemporary spirituality as part of an overarching collective manifestation of religion.[12] Owing to my professional location in the post-world-religions-paradigm study of religion, I see the category of spirituality as an important object of analysis for the discipline (see Mosurinjohn and Watts 2021). The case I am making is that it is *productive* to understand overload boredom as a spiritual crisis. Especially to the extent that we complicate the "individual" and "personal" language often associated with "spirituality" as "individual religion."[13] We must see the spiritual crisis as a collective affair.

Accordingly, I observe that overload boredom coincides with a cultural context where frameworks for pursuing connection with others, the wholeness of our psychic lives, truth, and meaning are threatened by a surplus of information, mediation, and the appearance of choice. I note, with the likes of Courtney Bender and Ann Taves (2012), that in this milieu, spirituality has become the idiom that bridges secular and religious concerns where matters of life meaning are concerned. Bender and Taves argue that we should consider spirituality as "a discursive practice that, in marking value, participates in its creation and, at the same time, highlights the felt need of many … to *expand* on the secular-religious binary when seeking to designate what matters" (8, emphasis mine). We must therefore resist the presumption that spirituality and religion are only ever opposite sides of the same coin (spirituality personal; religion collective) as much as we must resist the presumption that they are always inherently related. Likewise, we can see that the concept of boredom floats free of any necessary relation to particular religions or spiritualities, or to either religion or spirituality as a generic concept, but has been associated with fundamental existential concerns, whether in religious traditions, spiritual milieux, or secular contexts.

There is one final reason I will give for reuniting boredom with spiritual vocabularies of reflection. It is so difficult to write lucid, critical ontology, and so unfashionable, that as Jeffrey Kripal (2020) says, the humanities "are pushing a model of the human that is … so banal" it enervates us.[14] So I want to re-engage boredom as something that has to do with religion and spirituality because I want to put forward a less banal model of the human and human relation with the world. It is one that embraces the idea that "the general materialistic framework of the sciences at the moment is not wrong. It is simply half-right" (Kripal 2019, 12). And it is one that sees spirituality and religion as dealing with "the will to go away, to ignore, to be indifferent, blasé, bored" (Latour 2005, 36). Thinking boredom spiritually is a way of understanding it as a psychological, social, and ontological phenomenon that we can inquire about by exploring how it is bound up with the *desire* to make meaning within a mode of existence that not only seems void of it, but in which there really are growing fissures and gulfs between the individual, their interiority, and the world.

CHAPTER OUTLINE

My central argument is that there are resonances between overload boredom and historical incarnations of boredom as a spiritual crisis. I make this case in chapter 1, "A History of Boredom as a Spiritual Crisis," which grounds boredom as an existential problem related to social upheavals of meaning and temporality in the modern world.

In the second chapter I develop my theory of the disaffect of overload boredom in two parts. The first part of chapter 2 draws on theories of affect to critique the individual, piecemeal solutions to boredom contemporary pop-psychology presents. Doing so exposes the ways overload boredom acts disaffectively. It is the medium by which affects are flattened, but not destroyed. Overload boredom encourages the subject to withdraw from the world and themselves. To combat this withdrawal, I employ the speculative aesthetics[15] and enchanted materialism[16] of Jane Bennett and N. Katherine Hayles. Thinking materially with their speculative aesthetic probes affords time to feel the melancholy of withdrawal and to generate intimacy in relation to the objects of perception (sensory, affective, cognitive) hurtling through the screens of technological devices. The aesthetic-affective plays a receptive, attuning role that remediates the disaffect of overload boredom by seeing the subject and the object differently, yet as not so different from each other.

In chapter 3, "Habritual Texting: Why We Are Addicted to Boring Conversation," I develop a descriptive theory of how we tend to cope in the face of boredom as temporality. Habritual describes any communicative activity that we use to manage the pace of time and in so doing to manage our boredom. Sophia Le Fraga's video poem *W8ING* (2014), a take on Samuel Beckett's boredom play *Waiting for Godot*, serves as a paradigmatic example of the way that we repurpose boredom as a bonding tool and as a way to give new rhythms and meaning to the passage of time. *W8ING* unfolds the "waiting game" of texting as a series of text messages on an iPhone screen.

Examining *W8ING* reveals how using our information and communication technologies to alleviate boredom often ironically ends up reproducing the same conditions that bored us in the first place. It sheds new light on the way that people cling to stillness in a milieu of overload boredom, where information technology makes our affective connection to ourselves and others noisy and entropic, disturbing both psychic and collective individuation.

The concept of the "habitual" is descriptive, but it also begins to pose the more normative question: can boredom also be the solution to a crisis of meaning? Is it already being used that way? These questions I take up in chapter 4, "Uncertainty and Shared Entropy in Overload Culture." This chapter considers how all our voluntary "presencing" online and in social media speaks to the fact that although we do not want to be surveilled, we do want to be witnessed. This chapter uses the poem *i feel better after i type to you* (2006) by AOL user 23187425 and Thomas Claburn like a prism that refracts questions about the privacy risks we tolerate in order to get intimate with machines, make meaning out of information overload, and so process our boredom. *i feel better after i type to you* consists solely of hundreds of search queries from one user that were among the twenty million search records accidentally released by the company AOL in 2006. The writer Thomas Claburn noticed this set of stream-of-consciousness strings from one user that go on for hours a day over a period of weeks, yielding almost no search results at all. Two columns fill each page; on the right, the user's clipped observations, reports, and predictions, and on the left the time when the server logged each entry:

> 2006-05-12 01:01:13 yellow notice for cable
> 2006-05-12 01:01:37 joe did
> 2006-05-12 01:02:22 want miss tv
> 2006-05-12 01:03:22 had it put on basic cable
> 2006-05-12 01:04:06 did watch tv alot
> 2006-05-12 01:05:23 wal-mart 13" for 59.00
> 2006-05-12 01:06:33 i look at everything
> 2006-05-12 01:07:34 isle of black and white
> 2006-05-12 01:08:33 nice patio pillows
> 2006-05-12 01:09:11 not rain proof
> 2006-05-12 01:10:08 mean yes
> 2006-05-12 01:10:57 fit in my chairs
> 2006-05-12 01:11:34 go back over

2006-05-12 01:13:03 lowes has some red setting
2006-05-12 01:13:38 looking for four
2006-05-12 01:14:09 be here for life
2006-05-12 01:15:25 feel better after i type to you
2006-05-12 01:16:01 i feel better after i type to you

The title and the premise of *i feel better after i type to you* establishes an intimacy between human and information technology, allowing us to see the mutual exposure of human and machine actors to each other not just as an engine of overload, but as an attempt to cast our lot in common and develop a shared space. This chapter nuances the concept of overload boredom in terms of information theory – with respect to entropy, in particular, as a measurement of what is unknown or uncertain about a system. It argues that we need a theory of information to make sense of boredom as a problem of meaning, both to account for how information overload affects semantic and existential meaning, and to account for why and to what end we offer up so much of ourselves as data.

Chapter 5, "Information Enchantment: The Mystifying and the Kēdic," elaborates the concern with surveillance and "witness" raised in chapter four. It analyzes David Foster Wallace's *The Pale King* (2011), a novel about boredom in the IRS bureaucracy that has certain resonances with a tradition of conceptual art in which boredom's blankness has been both a subject and a canvas. Conceptual art has long had a close association with boredom (see Haladyn 2015) which has increasingly been related to information overload and the role of data in human life (e.g., Stephens 2015). As one character in *The Pale King* says: "True heroism is minutes, hours, weeks, year upon year of the quiet, precise, judicious exercise of probity and care – with no one there to see or cheer. This is the world … Routine, repetition, tedium, monotony, ephemeracy, inconsequence, abstraction, disorder, boredom" (Wallace 2011, 230–1). Here, the careful management of vast amounts of information is described as a spiritual vocation, one capable of wrestling with overload boredom in the vein of the monks of antiquity wrestling with the demon of boredom.

Dwelling on the boredom of the info-work sketched out in *The Pale King* reveals a definitive tension in the cultural context of overload and its technologies of production and consumption, which can be expressed in two idioms of enchantment. There is one form in which the boredom of laborious info-work presents a profound opportunity for relating to information in a way that encourages intimacy rather than withdrawal, and another in which information abundance, as a supposed consequence of the modern forces of rationalization, instead remains mystifying.

The conclusion (chapter 6) "Overload Boredom and a Hermeneutics of Care," summarizes the spiritual significance of twenty-first century overload boredom. The conclusions I draw from the studies in the previous chapters lead me to insist, in the final instance, that in choosing to form better relationships to information overload, we might access the generative side of boredom. At the same time as overload boredom attests an existential longing to relate to ourselves and to the world, it hides its spiritual significance. Recognizing it as a spiritual crisis will not give us immunity, but it does allow us to respond, rather than withdraw. Suggesting, perhaps, that the only way out of boredom, is to work carefully through.

I

A History of Boredom as a Spiritual Crisis

> In the day-to-day trenches of adult life, there is no such thing as atheism. There is no such thing as not worshipping. Everybody worships … But if you've really learned how to think, how to pay attention, then you will know you have other options. It will be within your power to experience a crowded, loud, slow, consumer-hell-type situation as not only meaningful but sacred, on fire with the same force that lit the stars – compassion, love, the sub-surface unity of all things. Not that that mystical stuff's necessarily true: the only thing that's capital-T True is that you get to decide how you're going to try to see it. You get to consciously decide what has meaning and what doesn't. You get to decide what to worship.
>
> David Foster Wallace, *This is Water: Some Thoughts, Delivered on a Significant Occasion, about Living a Compassionate Life*

In ordinary, contemporary thought, the idea of boredom does not have religious or spiritual connotations. Today, we have psychologists extolling "the upside of downtime" (Mann 2016; Baird, Smallwood et al. 2012), artists citing boredom as a precursor to creativity (e.g., Pirsig 1974),[1] mindfulness practitioners offering meditation as an antidote to distraction, and political revolutionaries advocating the political potential of slowing down (Berardi 2011). The fact that boredom raises fundamental questions, whose answers might disrupt the status quo, is why it is known as a creative state. But before the late modern era, boredom was also a spiritually significant state. A couple hundred years ago, boredom was a "synecdoche for the spiritual crisis" of modernity (Goodstein 2005, 224). And in pre-modern and modern accounts, boredom was painful, but meaningful. Historically, boredom was both cause and symptom of a productive spiritual struggle with tensions between cultural structure and individual choice, time spent on work versus leisure, and other definitive sites where subjectivity was cultivated and attachments to the world were formed.

The deepest history of boredom seems to originate in *akēdia*,[2] from late antiquity. Even then, the term had a "wide range of connotations, but boredom with the ascetic life was one of its principal senses" (Gale 2017). Akēdia signified boredom with the cultivation of subjectivity. Though the monks of the time situated akēdia "at the milder end of the more generic spectrum of *anxietas*," akēdia "led to an abandonment of concern for the self, and of the spiritual exercises ... that characterised it" (Gale 2017). Personifying akēdia as a demon, the monk Evagrius wrote:

> The demon of acedia – also called the noonday demon – is the one that causes the most serious trouble of all. He presses his attack upon the monk about the fourth hour and besieges the soul until the eighth hour. First of all he makes it seem that the sun barely moves, if at all, and that the day is fifty hours long. Then he constrains the monk to look constantly out of the windows, to walk outside the cell, to gaze carefully at the sun to determine how far it stands from the ninth hour, to look now this way and now that to see if perhaps [one of the brethren appears from his cell]. Then too he instils in the heart of the monk a hatred for the place, a hatred for his very life itself, a hatred for manual labour. He leads him to reflect that charity has departed from among the brethren, that there is no one to give encouragement. Should there be someone at this period who happens to offend him in some way or other, this too the demon uses to contribute further to his hatred. This demon drives him along to desire other sites where he can more easily procure life's necessities, more readily find work and make a real success of himself. He goes on to suggest that, after all, it is not the place that is the basis of pleasing the Lord. God is to be adored everywhere. He joins to these reflections the memory of his dear ones and of his former way of life. He depicts life stretching out for a long period of time, and brings before the mind's eye the toil of the ascetic struggle and, as the saying has it, leaves no leaf unturned to induce the monk to forsake his cell and drop out of the fight. No other demon follows close upon the heels of this one (when he is defeated) but only a state of deep peace and inexpressible joy arise out of this struggle. (Gale 2017)

This vignette displays all the elements common to the many definitions of boredom grounding this book: boredom has to do with time in the world and in human interiority; has both metaphysical and sociohistorical dimensions; and has to do with our existential orientation to the world. Most distinctively, boredom is a warping of time and a breakdown of meaning that, left unchecked, can throw a spanner into the very shape and aim of existence. The sociohistorical conditions and metaphysical frameworks belonging to existential cultures of late antiquity, early modernity, and late modernity are vastly different. Yet, boredom is a powerful affective site for grappling with the spiritual crisis of each.

Despite the diagnostic power boredom offers, and its importance for understanding the affective landscape of the twentieth century, there are relatively few modern theories of boredom. However, understanding the dominant modern theories of boredom will help contextualize my project, showing both what it owes to twentieth century boredom and the work it inspired, and how it departs from it. My departure is not only "theoretical" – I am not looking to improve upon past theory, but rather, to show that the boredom itself has changed. One sees this not only in art and memoir, but perhaps more sharply, in attempts to articulate boredom in a philosophical or theoretical frame. For this reason, I will turn now to giving a history of modern theories of boredom in this chapter before developing my account of contemporary overload boredom in the next.

BOREDOM IN THE TWENTIETH CENTURY

Heidegger's Theory of Boredom

The twentieth century philosopher who I think makes the most interesting claims about boredom is Martin Heidegger.[3] He makes the paradoxes of boredom explicit: boredom is both noxious and precious, both objective and subjective, both trivial and profound. Heidegger ([1929/30] 1995) gave us the idea that boredom is, in fact, the fundamental mood of the modern times (157), meaning his moment of twentieth century modernity. But boredom for Heidegger actually springs directly from the temporality of our being-in-the-world (127). Simply put, boredom exists in relation between the way the world is set up and the way human mind/bodies are set up. Like a scent on the air, there is something about boredom that is all around us and to which we each have a different kind of sensitivity. Boredom is an affect that circulates, is contagious in certain circumstances, and catches us up in it.

Heidegger also gives us the idea that there are three types of boredom. The first is the most superficial, and it is where one "becomes bored by" something (127). Being bored-by involves the need to drive away time. His paradigmatic example of this kind of boredom is waiting for a train. Second, there is the deeper "being bored with" (127) that describes what appears, in retrospect, to have been a waste of time. This is like a dinner party, which, on reflection, was superficial and pretentious. For Heidegger this is an existentially more significant form of boredom than the first, because we participated in something inauthentic and we therefore abandoned a little part of ourselves in order to do it. Then, third, there is the most profound boredom expressed by the impersonal phrase "it is boring for one" (134). In this state, which is achieved merely by a deepening of the lighter varieties of boredom, it is "hopeless" to try passing the time (136). When there is no hope of passing the time, we are forced to confront something fundamental about the world and ourselves. In Heidegger's words: "to not permit any passing the time means to let this boredom become overpowering … the 'it is boring for one' – this *it is thus for one* – has in itself *this* character of *manifesting how things stand concerning us*. This attunement brings us ourselves into the possibility of an *exceptional understanding*" (136).

In profound boredom, we have a moment of reckoning with what the world offers and what we bring to it, and how we will choose to interpret the meaning of those endowments and deficits. We see that there is no intrinsic meaning to life, so we are called to make one. We can experience our freedom and agency by taking responsibility for this process. Heidegger touted "profound boredom" as an experience of time stilled, wherein the collapse of past, present, and future held the germ of contemplation – and therefore the potential of self-knowledge ([1929/30] 1995). Moments of profound boredom are therefore moments of great "vision" (Biceaga 2006, 149). Interpreting Heidegger, Victor Biceaga argues "not having the possibility to pass the time means that [the human being] temporalizes itself in such a way that every present is pregnant with new possibilities carrying forward the heritage of the past" (146). It is here, in this kind of meditative, creatively charged state, that we are primed to appreciate the it-could-be-otherwise-ness of everything. It can therefore be an empowering state of being, where we are standing in a reflective relation to time instead of being rushed along with it.

The Paradox of Free Choice and "Oppressiveness" in Boredom

Heidegger saw boredom as an existential orientation that structures the experience of modern subjects. For Heidegger, moods "always co-present objects and they do so by giving them a horizon and arranging them into a world" (Biceaga 2006, 143). Moods, therefore, are a way in which we are outside ourselves – they link the subjective and the objective. Heidegger considered boredom as an essential mood of modern people. Boredom was the fundamental mood of modernity because modern people no longer *needed* anything in particular. The modern individual had *freedom to* choose their allegiances but also had *freedom from* any unbreakable ties:

> The absence of an essential oppressiveness in Dasein [the experience of being in the world that is peculiar to human beings] is the emptiness as a whole, so that no one stands with anyone else and no community stands with any other in the rooted unity of essential action. Each and every one of us are servants of slogans, adherents to a program, but none is the custodian of the inner greatness of Dasein and its necessities (*Bedrängnis*). This being left empty (*Leergelassenheit*) ultimately resonates in our Dasein, its emptiness is the absence of any essential oppressiveness. The mystery is lacking in our Dasein, and thereby the inner terror that every mystery carries with it and that gives Dasein its greatness remains absent. The absence of oppressiveness is what fundamentally oppresses and leaves us most profoundly empty, i.e., the *fundamental emptiness that bores us*. This absence of oppressiveness is only apparently hidden; it is rather attested by the very activities with which we busy ourselves in our contemporary restlessness. (Heidegger 163–4)

Without the enabling constraints of traditional structures in work, family, religion, and community, our commitments seem arbitrary. Of course, unless you take some kind of radically teleological stance that assumes an ultimate meaning *sub specie aeternitatis*, our commitments *are* arbitrary in the sense that social and cultural meanings have a human authorship, collective though it may be. At any rate, Heidegger's point is that, although boredom is a dimension of the time-constituting absolute flow of consciousness and is therefore always with us, it especially prevails in the modern "absence of oppressiveness."

When any number of ways of being in the world seem plausible, the result is existential skepticism. The historian Elizabeth Goodstein (2005) interprets modern boredom as an affective manifestation of the democratization of modern existential skepticism. The point here is to emphasize that while boredom is a capacity of all human beings since we are beings-in-time, there are social reasons why modern times elicit the expression of this capacity more than previous times and are amplified in our twenty-first century modes of being.

It is not necessarily that the activities novel to twenty-first-century life are inherently boring and ought to be condemned, but that the technologies of social media are structured to *make* us busy and restless with them. Busyness, drama, and crisis must be constantly renewed because they are not embedded in shared systems of meaning that give them any significance outside themselves. The reason why busyness, drama, and crisis are problematic is not that they are inherently bad, but because when they are only a means to an end of *simulating* an "essential oppressiveness," or, in other words, simulating the enabling constraint needed for the human being to experience existential meaning. (We will see in chapters 4, 5, and 6 how some artists have developed certain enabling constraints to deal with this problem, which range from temporary aesthetic strategies to comprehensive philosophies of life).

Given that Heidegger's account laments the anesthetizing effects of boredom on the uprooted individual in an alienating world, it would seem that the kind of boredom that grips "the modern times" corresponds better to the superficial being-bored-by than to the deeper or profound levels of boredom. But Heidegger never completed his analysis of time, which figured boredom as the "eternal now." Enter the French philosopher and sociologist Henri Lefebvre.

Lefebvre's Theory of Boredom

Lefebvre ([1961] 2002; [1962] 1995) saw the creative potential of boredom, much as Heidegger did, but its value for him was revolutionary. For the Marxist Lefebvre, boredom could be an "aleatory moment." The "aleatory" (which Lefebvre draws from Althusser, via Marx), is the "becoming-necessary of the encounter of contingencies" (Althusser 2006, 194). He proclaimed: "Between the world which is chock-a-block full of realism and positivism, and the gaping world of pure negativity and nihilism, our aim is to discover the open world, the world of what is possible" (Lefebvre [1961] 2002, 263). But the time of boredom was not always a positive one in Lefebvre's thinking, because it was a time potentiated by a host of Sisyphean modern inventions including the toil of routinized and subspecialized labour under the alternating acceleration and torpidity of universal clock time. For Lefebvre, boredom is an experience of time as abstract, linear, sequential, predictable, and monotonous (Gardiner 2012, 44). No doubt this is why he was confident in diagnosing boredom as a "mass epidemic." Lefebvre did not need a sociological survey filled with self-reports of who was bored; he understood that time itself had changed. In the modern factory, the assembly line worker is not only alienated from the fruits of their labour, but also set outside of communal time and therefore alienated from their species-being.[4] Life used to unfold according to the intrinsic time-scales of natural cycles like seasons and life stages. In contrast, under the eye of the clock, which is itself an information technology, the worker's life is remoulded in accordance with abstract, linear, universal clock time.

On account of the switch from communal to linear commodity time, Lefebvre highlights a cascade of boredom that we can see in corrosive aesthetic, social, and cultural effects. The clock time of capitalist production results in a "growing multiplicity of neutral, indifferent instants" ([1981] 2005, 85). As the symbols of the group become less salient, mechanical repetition deadens the senses, and they become attuned instead to what Michael Gardiner (2012) calls the monosemantic "signal." Signals, he says, "reduce the semantic field to a fixed image or idea, and interrupt the continuity of historical experience and collective memorialization" (Gardiner 2012, 44). The plausibility of any one worldview, especially a supernaturally ordered one where everyone was in their God-given place, was challenged on a mass scale as the effects of the Scientific Revolution, the Enlightenment, and the Industrial Revolution rippled through people's lives. Only the signal – mere information, rather than existential meaning – was universally on offer to take its place. This is why, according to Goodstein: "'Boredom' epitomizes the dilemma of the subject for whom enlightenment and scientific progress have caused, in Max Weber's term, the 'disenchantment' of the world, yet it comes to be lived as a pseudo-religious revelation of the ultimate meaninglessness of existence" (Goodstein 2005, 4).[5] Existential skepticism leads to the intuition of the ultimate meaninglessness of existence, which is what provokes the spiritual crisis identified with modern boredom.

However, as shown above, it is clear that a totalizing experience of boredom is not the inevitable consequence of disenchantment (re: Weber's *Protestant Work Ethic and the Spirit of Capitalism*). Of course, not everybody "lost" religion, but the function of religion changed. It could no longer be taken for granted as a ground for one's sense of self in relation to the world (the loss of what Peter Berger [1979] called "plausibility structures"). In this sense, boredom, as the intellectual and affective sensibility of existential meaninglessness, therefore became part of the way modern people oriented themselves.

But what we can see with twenty-first century overload boredom is that now we are actually much closer to Heidegger's diagnosis of boredom as the fundamental mood of modernity. Now, overload has gone both micro and macro. In info-capitalism, attention is still cheap, but it is also now the main commodity. Whereas the clock used to be on the factory wall, now the time-tracking devices are in sight all the time. Time-keeping technologies used to set a boundary between labour and leisure in daily life. Now the individual is responsible for time-keeping in every aspect of life and the goal is to see how it can be maximized – overloaded. What was capitalism's push to maximize the time of production, now has gotten internalized into how much more of myself can I produce in this time. And the human experiential present cannot compare with the algo-rhythmic time of the computer. We have gone from technologies of external production to technologies of internal production. The faster and fuller we get internally, the less capable we are of producing the slowness and stillness we need to reflect, integrate, and create, and so the overload short circuits the human being's reflexive capacities for meaning-making. Recently, philosopher Lars Svendsen ([1999] 2008, 135) even ventured to consider whether "perhaps time now passes so quickly that it will swallow up boredom." I do not think it will, but the temporality of overload boredom is a stark contrast to that of older boredoms, especially that which the philosopher Walter Benjamin[6] called "traditional boredom."

Benjamin's Theory of "Traditional" versus Modern Boredom

Benjamin identified traditional boredom in his 1936 "The Storyteller," with being able to tell and absorb narratives. This "being bored in a 'good' way" is a matter of repetition. This repetition is not like that of the factory line, which brings numbing habituation and tedium. The temporality of traditional boredom is a relaxed and ancestral one. To repeat is to recreate. Repetition holds out the promise of immersive focus. Traditional boredom is a state of receptivity where small sparks of imagination can be fanned into life gently. Overload boredom extinguishes those sparks like a heavy wind. Benjamin's notion of boredom as a state of "mental relaxation" is clearly not a state of being-bored-by or being-bored-with a story. It is therefore a mode of genuine boredom that awakens the being to its presence there in the light of Being. As a state of creativity and receptivity, boredom is seen to invite meaning making. But, compared with its role in traditional societies, it is hard to achieve amidst the distraction of modern capitalist ones. It was this "atrophy of experience," as Benjamin called it, that ruined the possibility of the relaxing boredom.[7] The rhythms of premodern life, like rites of passage and seasonal time cycles, were replaced by standardized clock time, mass-produced commodities, and other forms of sameness. Correspondingly, experience and the time it takes fell in value compared to commodities and commodity time.

Yet the reign of capitalist production time also meant that a modicum of leisure time had also become widely available, and the moral burden of using it well became palpable. Before this, boredom's precursors – like akēdia, *ennui*, melancholy, and *Langeweile* – tended to be available only to religious devouts and economic elites. This was boredom as luxury, sometimes eliding into boredom as decadence and sin. In modernity, the subject for whom boredom became a definitive dilemma was the autonomous liberal subject. Born of an "Enlightenment-era" context "infused with tacit Protestant presuppositions," this is also the same subject who came to have individual subjective belief, which came to be identified as the defining feature of (a disenchanted) religion (which must be replaced with some new "revelation") (Bender and Taves 2012, 14). This subject, for the first time, *expected life to be interesting* in the sense of being personally meaningful. "In the mid-century discourse on this experience without qualities [boredom], the weight of human responsibility for producing and guiding … progress comes into awareness. The ambivalent desire for a rapidly impending future gives rise to an idiom of reflection in which the moral burden of time that must be used and not wasted becomes palpable" (Goodstein 2005, 127). Thus, the experience of modern boredom was thus partly made possible by its opposite, "interest," which only came into widespread use around the same time and with the same frequency as the word boredom did. Before that time, the term "interesting" designated something of objective importance, but in the modern sense, what was interesting became as subjective as what was boring.

Unlike akēdia, which indicated a problem with the *self*, modern boredom diagnosed a problem with the *world* and its failure to interest through experience, which became the responsibility of the individual to deal with. As Goodstein (2005, 99) writes, "the contemporary terror of boredom, which testifies to its apparent inevitability, is saturated with the post-romantic resignation to a world in which neither work nor leisure can bring happiness to subjects who no longer hope for divine restitution in the next."[8] On account of the weakening of shared meaning structures and the availability of technologies of self-making (education; information technologies; leisure-time hobbies), people had to shoulder the responsibility themselves to make life meaningful and interesting.

INTERSECTIONS OF TWENTIETH AND TWENTY-FIRST CENTURY BOREDOM

Modern theories of boredom took boredom to be about both the subjectivity of the individual and the fragmentation of the collective, about both the temporality of the human and the temporality of capitalism. Theories like Heidegger's show us the capacity for profound boredom is a universal, timeless one insofar as the human being "is time and boredom is one possible expression of time" (Svendsen [1999] 2008, 125). But this framing does not take into account that not everyone gets to experience it the same. In order to frame the particular cultural context under examination in this book, I will now explore how identity markers such as race, class, disability, gender, and other ways of categorizing citizenship and humanity come into experiences of boredom, and whether boredom is read onto a subject, so as to specify what my theory of overload boredom can and cannot account for, and to justify the value of what it does.

Let us begin by situating the philosophy I have worked with most in this chapter, that of Heidegger. The disadvantage of Heidegger's framing of boredom is that although it treats boredom as a cultural mood, it still ends up being more about the individual's psychological capacity for boredom than the way the cultural mood affects differently situated beings. In Heidegger's thinking, the modern subject for whom boredom was definitive was the autonomous liberal subject. Moreover, although some philosophers (e.g., Derrida 1987) have characterized "his vocabulary and his network of metaphors ... [as being] the same as those of the era's ostensibly liberal thinkers" (Brody 2014), others (e.g., Faye 2009) have noted that Heidegger "speaks in his 'Black Notebooks' of the 'worldlessness' of Judaism" and we discover "that the Heideggerian idea of 'being-in-the-world' which is central to 'Being and Time' can take on the meaning of a discriminatory term with an anti-Semitic intent" (Faye in Brody 2014). It is thus not incidental that Heidegger's theory does not take into account how boredom manifests uniquely in different bodies with their own mix of psychological boredoms and social oppressions and privileges, or how they got that way. As Sara Ahmed (2006; via Lefebvre) points out about Heidegger's notion of how beings come to be in the world, no one and nothing is simply "thrown," appearing altogether in a moment; "an arrival takes time, and the time that it takes shapes 'what' it is that arrives" (40).

For example, the bored housewife may just as well reach a profound level of reflection on the meaning of her life as a professional philosopher, and what matters in general, on account of repeatedly facing the burdens of caregiving and physical domestic labour (see Friedan 1963). Only, repetition of that labour makes her physical work disappear, and heteropatriarchal and racial capitalism is oriented away from her reflective work, so her boredom probably will not be awarded the dignity of the suffering artist type. Thus, as Ahmed reminds us: "It is important that we think ... about how the repetition of actions takes us in certain directions: we are also orientating ourselves toward some objects more than others, including not only physical objects ... but also objects of thought, feeling, and judgment, as well as objects in the sense of aims, aspirations, and objectives" (56). So, we can ask: what happens when her acts of reflection are "not reproduced as a masculine domain by the collective repetition of such moments of deviation?" (61). As Allison Pease (2012) has shown, women's boredom in modernist literature served as an emblem for a feminist critique of women's social sidelining and as a literary device for asserting their will. But this deviance was supported by the significance awarded to boredom by the larger masculine-coded modernist literary culture. Today, in the Internet age when "boredom is a crime,"[9] the bored housewife has a different significance as a cultural trope. To be a bored housewife is first of all a matter of class privilege; the bored housewife now gets her own reality TV show, as in the Real Housewives franchise. Yet this class privilege does not carry the same cultural capital as the boredom of the ennui-drenched aesthete languishing on a divan.[10] Nor can the boredom of the contemporary housewife stand in for feminine gendered boredom broadly; in offscreen reality, most women will be either working or feeling the pressure to get enough work to make ends meet. In info-capitalist North America, women are as likely to be digital workers and consumers as men.

Differing levels of precarity determine how much, if any, time there is to reflect and to sink into the affects of boredom. There is no time when there is immediate and overwhelming threat to life. A stark example of this occurring on a mass scale is anti-Black and anti-Indigenous racist violence, especially through policing. The survivors of such violence must face frequent crisis without, as Henrika McCoy (2020) writes of herself and her Black colleagues "the luxury of resting." Yet crisis, over time, morphs into extreme weariness and exhaustion, and it would be a mistake to ignore the profound reflective dimension of this state.

In these contexts, Sianne Ngai's concept of "stuplimity," a combination of boredom with shock, would be a better suited than "overload boredom" for calling attention to the mixture of shock and exhaustion produced and sustained by the reality for BIPOC social media users scrolling through updates from the front lines of these conflicts on, for example, #BlackTwitter. Ngai writes that: "To refer to the aesthetic experience in which astonishment is paradoxically united with boredom as stuplimity … allows us to invoke the sublime – albeit negatively, since we infuse it with thickness or even stupidity – while detaching it from its spiritual and transcendent connotations and its close affiliation with Romanticism … What constitutes stuplimity … [is] a concatenation of boredom and astonishment – a bringing together of what 'dulls' and what 'irritates' or agitates; of sharp, sudden excitation and prolonged desensitization, exhaustion, or fatigue." Digitally engaging the racial reckoning in the era of Black Lives Matter, Truth and Reconciliation Commission, and the rise of anti-Asian violence during the COVID pandemic involves BIPOC digital media users holding the agitating affects of racial trauma together with the dulling affects of comparing this to the "heaven" of avocado toast and inspirational quotes incorrectly attributed to Martin Luther King of what comedian Bo Burnham satirizes as "White Woman's Instagram."

The boredom of Heidegger cannot make sense of this as part of a cultural mood of boredom. But my theory of overload boredom can because overload boredom is a phenomenon of the rapid pace of incoming information, the demands of self-making, and relating to others through social media unique to the twenty-first century. A theory of overload boredom will allow us to appreciate how these individually situated psychological experiences of boredom are informed by a social world of information, technology, and choice overload. The theory of overload boredom makes it possible to track boredom in relation to the extent that information and media technologies organize lives, differently situated as they are. Overload boredom is an affect of global capitalism, a fundamentally inequality-producing, white supremacist, and heteropatriarchal system. Drawing on Ahmed's reading of Heidegger in *Queer Phenomenology* (2006), we can say that info-capitalism is oriented toward whiteness, cis-hetero-maleness, able-bodiedness, and wealth, and it achieves the reproduction of these particular forms by putting white objects, cis-hetero-male objects, etc. closer, while other objects become non-perceivable.

This is powerfully illustrated by Sarah Sharma's work on the "chronopolitics" of this system. Info-capitalism produces an "uneven cultural politics of time," in Sharma's (2014, 7) phrase, where people's different relationships to labour, leisure, and even longevity, configure their experience of time. Those "whose labor is explicitly oriented toward negotiating time and the time of others" (Sharma 2014, 15) are divided into different, interdependent groups. These groups of individuals experience different "temporal architectures" designed to manage their time. Those privileged groups whose temporalities are particularly valued such as business travellers, have their time enhanced by expedited travel clearances, frequent flyer lounges where they can exercise, wash, rest, and eat, and boutique hotels equipped with lamps radiating the right frequencies to help jet-lagged bodies wake up for work. The material stuff that enables the temporalities of these privileged groups are made possible by the labour of devalued groups, such as taxi drivers, whose time is exploited to "make time" for business travellers rushing from one meeting or airport to the next. In the service of these travellers, taxi drivers must recalibrate their circadian clock, which communicates to the rest of the brain and body not just whether it is time to sleep or wake, but a whole raft of physiological mechanisms crucial to basic human health, such as whether metabolism should be high or metabolism should be low. Taxi drivers, in other words, are expected to mortgage their health, their bodies, as a condition of their labour. Phenomenology of time "exposes the 'sedimentation' of history in the repetition of bodily action" (Ahmed 2006, 56, via Judith Butler).

With respect to boredom in info-capitalism, there is a different temporal architecture determining the experience of speed, attention, and stimulation for people cast right out of the institutions of the family and the labour economy. As Bruce O'Neill (2017) shows of those left homeless by the failures of global capitalism and the state, there is no way to participate in a society organized around production and consumption, so boredom is an enduring struggle in everyday life. O'Neill demonstrates in his ethnography in the Romanian capital of Bucharest how the transition from Eastern European socialism to Western European capitalism displaced people from circuits of consumption and production, and into a "space of boredom." For these dispossessed, boredom is an "acidic inner state marked by the pronounced lack of even mundane distractions" (120).

Bucharestians in homeless shelters, day centres, and public parks are searching for stimulation, but have not the digital means to do so in this "infrastructure of displacement" (69). Neither personal digital devices nor the publics they interface with are part of their temporal architectures. Their stories of spiritual crisis go largely unnoticed in the cultural processes of meaning-making that tick along without them. Even as they bring overload boredom, "Internet portals proliferating on the glossy surfaces of phones, watches, and eyeglasses … offer the promise, for those who can afford them, not only of staying informed and connected but also of being always able to escape" (182). Boredom "grinds down on the global economy's most peripheral populations" in a different way than it does for the workers-cum-commodities I am focused on in this book.

The fast and the slow of privileged and marginalized people's temporalities constitute and are constituted by material realities. I see overload boredom as a consequence of the way information and choice show up in this temporality. Hence, the often-assumed link between digital media and speed-up remains a key tie to unpick in our analysis of how global info-capitalism involves both "speed-up" and "slow-down" as means of biopolitical social control.

In this, I build on Heidegger's distinction between superficial boredom and profound boredom. In the next chapter, I show how the overload of information and choice works against deepening, or furthering possibility for meaning-making within the lighter varieties of boredom insofar as an individual embodies dealing with overload – to the extent, in other words, that the twenty-first century worker-cum-commodity can or must consume and produce information and media, especially as part of the project of self-making. I will show that the phenomenological time of this info-media activity is both fast and slow, and that from a philosophical perspective, the formal properties of the condition of overload conduce to the same sorts of meaning – and time- and world-disclosing realizations as the personal experience of profound boredom. That is, the condition of overload itself can be looked at as a site that embodies profound boredom. Given the foregoing examination of situated forms of boredom about which my theory of overload boredom does not generalize, I recognize that the temporal architectures of many people's lives will not be orientated toward this philosophical perspective. Nonetheless, I am putting this book out into a world it says something about: the recasting of old power relations as relations of exchange is an uneven phenomenon – it is different for the pauper and for the king – but it is a globalizing one, and what these capital relations value is increasingly time, attention, and information.

In the crash site of meaning, trapped underneath wrecked symbols and broken patterns, we may find a way out by taking familiar material and recycling it – an aleatory moment of repetition and difference – into new cultural forms. I take boredom as a critical theme for making sense of the competing pulls and imperatives that compose subjectivity today to encourage the subject to reject totalizing demands on their attention, and instead figure out how we might relate to meaning, and making something meaningful, in a culture of overload. Yet overload boredom, as an effect of info-capitalism, and the broader media ecology of ubiquitous connection and accelerating inputs, cannot be allowed to dictate the terms of everyday life. But what I heuristically call its *spiritual significance* may be recuperated.[11]

2

The Disaffect of Overload Boredom

> Maybe dullness is associated with psychic pain because something that's dull or opaque fails to provide enough stimulation to distract people from some other, deeper type of pain that is always there, if only in an ambient, low-level way, and which most of us spend nearly all our time and energy trying to distract ourselves from feeling, or at least from feeling directly or with our full attention. Admittedly, the whole thing's pretty confusing, and hard to talk about abstractly … but surely something must lie behind not just Muzak in dull or tedious places any more but now also actual TV in waiting rooms, supermarkets' checkouts, airport gates, SUVs' backseats. Walkman, iPods, BlackBerries, cell phones that attach to your head. This terror of silence with nothing diverting to do.
>
> David Foster Wallace, *The Pale King*

Modern boredom was born of democratization of existential skepticism, and new proto-informational technologies like the factory clock. Modern boredom preceded overload, which happens when happens when there is no time of the day and no corner of the earth where productive time is not ticking, when the only time we have is for self-production. The burden facing those of us who can only live in productive time is to locate our worth outside of the relationship between the degree of effort we put in and what we think we deserve because of it. And making meaningful leisure is ever more fraught as both the work and products of capitalism leave us overwhelmed and enervated. In an age dominated by information and communication technologies, connection has not been an easy answer to the problem of alienation from a shared moral universe, from our work, and from other people. In fact, perhaps this being "alone together" (Turkle 2011) is even worse because the expectation of connectedness is so in conflict with reality. This problem exposes the digital heart that has late modern boredom beating its new, tachycardic rhythm.

My intention in this chapter is to make the case for attending to dimensions of boredom we would not otherwise be able to acknowledge or discuss unless we use frameworks that can admit of the passing-beneath-mention dimensions of emotion and sensation. In the first half of this chapter I describe overload boredom as a "disaffective medium" that suffuses the subjective-collective assemblage. In the second half of this chapter, I show how we can use aesthetic-affective techniques from speculative realism for considering the "alien" parts of the world and our own experience, and the withdrawal between them that is signified by the spiritual crisis of overload boredom.

Throughout the twenty-first century, especially since the digital revolution and the Internet, the popular discourse around boredom has been a trivial one. For many people, boredom appears as some version of the "simple" boredom that a child might feel on a rainy day, vastly different than the akēdia of ancient monks, or the aesthete lounging in melancholia. We are now unlikely to give meaning to our boredom in relation to "demonically inspired religious doubt" or in terms of the "physiological cum cosmological" (Gardiner 2012, 40). Today boredom seems not only unimportant, but unbelievable: how could we be bored when there are so many ways to connect and so much to do? As I write this paragraph, a Zoom call, a phone call, several text messages, and five emails are coming in. So how could I be bored? I have a lot of things to do and people to connect with. So many, in fact that my attention is scattered across them so that I am engaging with each more superficially than I would like. I am free to choose where my attention goes, but I feel an implicit demand to attend to all of these things and people, and more or less *now*. I feel the brain fog move in as the waste of the thinking I have done clouds the thinking I am trying to do. I want to attend to all of these tasks and people, but I begin to feel defeatist about my ability to do so. I am not sure whether there are demons here, but my foggy mind lacks the depth of melancholia; it is flat, like the screens of my devices, and arbitrary. This is overload boredom.

As shown in the previous chapter, boredom can be caused not just by too little stimulation, but also by too much – too much information to parse for meaning, too much connectivity to engage with any one connection, too many choices to do anything other than stand before them, paralyzed. The cognitive demands of this twenty-first-century informational, social, and economic environment are enormous, producing affective and cognitive pressures from all directions. One source is the capitalist pressure to consume. In *Does Ethics Have a Chance in a World of Consumers?*, Zygmunt Bauman describes the latent message of late capitalist culture[1] as "Hurry up – there's no time to waste" (2008, 145). Yet, "whatever your gain" from promptly consuming the latest trend, "it won't last forever. Whatever insurance for safe sailing you acquire will need to be renewed once the 'coming months' pass" (145). Even leisure becomes a kind of work that is never done.

And then, there is the work of wage labour. For many, cognitive labour has become the main tool for production in today's info-capitalist economy, rather than the material labour of standing on the factory line pulling the same lever endlessly. Cognitive labour is touted by corporations as a good thing because it allows workers to exercise their creativity, imagination, and freedom. The flip side of involving the whole being of the worker, though, is that work becomes part of the whole being. The boundaries between labour and leisure blur from both sides. People use the same technologies of work for pleasure, and inhabit the hyperreal world of the spectacle in both spheres. "The very affective and emotional registers of our lives" come to be "shaped fundamentally by [these] transformations in the productive process now unfolding in the technologically-advanced societies of the global North" (Gardiner 2014, 29). Accordingly, these transformations shape a kind of boredom different from that of the factory line. It is more pernicious. It comes from the "hermeneutical nihilism" of info-capitalism (ibid., 45) where the overload of information threatens to annihilate meaning and the very process of meaning-making itself. To make meaning in one's life is, after all, a type of productivity, but one that is devalued in our hyper-connected digital information age.

In *Homo Deus*, Yuval Harari writes: "Modernity is a deal … The entire contract can be summarised in a single phrase: humans agree to give up meaning in exchange for power" (2017, 233). This formulation disarticulates meaning from power, and this captures something essential about an era where humans' relationships to each other have been widely reconfigured in quantity and quality, and so have their ontological relationships to the world. But perhaps we could think of power in Harari's formula as a matter of humans affecting others and the world without the reciprocal sense of being affected by them. Power then, is not what is exchanged for meaning, but a pivot between meaning and boredom, or better yet, an axis along which meaning and boredom lie at opposite ends. We can then think of overload boredom as varying with greater or lesser access to sites of reciprocal influence – greater or lesser power. This is what the philosopher and psychologist Anna Ciaunica (2018) describes as happening in experiences of depersonalization or derealization: "Perhaps the feeling of being fully and properly alive, then, depends on … mov[ing] seamlessly between the objective and subjective points of view. In phenomenological terms, we might say that we shift back and forth across the bridge between the external realm of *Körper/Leben* [the physical, organic object of the body] and the internal one of *Leib/Erleben [the first-person perspective from inside the body]*. When it is functioning well, this experiential openness remains tacit and imperceptible, even as it pervades and sustains almost everything we do. But when we lose the link … the feeling of inhabiting reality itself also slips away."

The sundering of an individual's felt sense of self in the world reveals the unrelenting acceleration of what Franco Berardi calls "the info-sphere – the environment from which information arrives in your brain" (2011). The sheer volume of input channelled into subjects of the "information society" can be overwhelming rather than formative. Our brains are amazingly plastic ("explosively" plastic, in Catherine Malabou's [2007] phrase) but overload exceeds and undermines this plasticity. As Berardi (2011) ominously puts it: "Do not forget that your brain functions in time, and needs time in order to give attention and understanding. But attention cannot be infinitely accelerated … You can accelerate attention by taking amphetamines, for instance, or using other techniques or drugs that give you the possibility of being more attentive, more productive in the field of attention. But you know how it ends." With the acceleration of information plus the blurring of boundaries between labour and leisure, our capacity to parse information and to make choices based on it is stretched to the point of fraying. Overload boredom is thus a political feeling related to the exigencies of living in a certain kind of political, economic, and social order. Overload of various kinds can function as a hegemonic tool to induce apathy in publics – overwork, overchoice, oversaturation in images. Indeed, we could say that the overload boredom of life under info-capitalism *disaffects* individuals. And yet, this disaffection goes beyond the individual liberal, autonomous, subject and their objects of labour and leisure. Thinking affecognitively,[2] overload boredom is, as

M. Gail Hamner writes, not so much a psychological state as it is "an interpersonal matrix of expectation *in the very moment of its unexpected disruption*" (Hamner 2018b, 95). The concept of overload boredom indexes these ruptures of our connection to ourselves and others in ways that do not disintegrate the connections, but make them noisy and entropic, disturbing both psychic and collective individuation and therefore the very collective itself.

DIS/AFFECT

In order to understand boredom, let us flip the script of scholars who typically use affect to get at "the social, material, life-fueling buzz" (Supp-Montgomerie 2015, 343), and instead look at the ways that "life-fueling buzz" is dampened and dulled. The problem this helps resolve is that boredom persists in being identified with the *disappearance* of affect, particularly in work that examines the phenomenology of boredom. This work often falls back on tropes of negation. Martin Hand (2016), for instance, describes the streamlined activities of the digital social world as "indicative of a loss of empathy and affect," concluding that "such a loss of affect ultimately produces digital boredom" (122). I agree with Hand's point that, when our computers and smartphones can do so much, the many activities that take place through them take on a similar flatness of experience. We hold the same device, consume information that conforms to the same display capabilities, and repeatedly update our social media accounts, if indeed we want to be "present" in the digital social world. However, overload boredom is not a loss or disappearance of affect; overload boredom *disaffects*. It is the medium by which affects are flattened.

Overload boredom disaffects the life-fueling buzz filling the vestiges, spandrels, and negative space of material and embodied vibration. It appears as flat affect, detachment, and other contemporary post-melodramatic subjectivity. Overload boredom, construed as something disaffective is not an *absence*, it is present and active in that it mediates affect on all levels, and more interestingly, on the level of the collective – the "interpersonal matrix." Overload boredom could be construed as "the collective body-mind's way of warning of us the need to slow things down … in an increasingly digitalised, posthuman world" (Gardiner 2014, 44). But how to intervene on the *collective* body-mind (or mind|body, in my own formulation)? The strategies on offer for dealing with overload tend to be overwhelmingly individual.

Re-examining Boredom in Contemporary Popular Psychology

Framing overload boredom as a *disaffective medium* allows us to reevaluate tropes popularized from the psychology of boredom, specifically in mindfulness and self-help discourses. Psychology, and the popular science writers who draw on it, sees boredom primarily in the realm of individuals managing their emotions. In fact, it seems that in most popular boredom psychology discourses, emotion is confined inside the individual body, it is not an affective structure belonging to the collective socio-political body. Pop-science ignores the wider boredom studies literature and instead tends to cherry pick the psychology research on boredom and attention and cast it in self-help terms of boredom avoidance. This reinforces the stereotype that "boredom" is having "nothing to do," not anything close to what I have identified as overload boredom. Ironically, these popularizers and the people who follow their advice are contributing to the very disaffective properties of overload boredom itself. For one thing, they advocate techniques for self-making that are not about making meaning, but about optimizing for the "digitalised posthuman world" by beating boredom. And second, they make it harder to recognize overload boredom in the first place, by framing boredom as a matter of "nothing to do," when in fact, there is already too much to do, and these popularizers intensify this by giving us more to do, more cognitive levers to pull.

Case in point, the study reported in The American Association for the Advancement of Science's (AAAS) story "People Would Rather Be Electrically Shocked than Left Alone with Their Thoughts" (Whitehead 2014). This story relayed the findings of Wilson et al.'s (2014) study "Just Think: The Challenges of the Disengaged Mind," which sought to understand the emotional effects of deliberate inward-directed thought. "Just Think" deals with many factors in boredom: time, meaning, choice, information, attention, and aloneness. Presiding over the AAAS story was an image of St John, gazing apathetically down from Hieronymus Bosch's painting *Saint John the Baptist in the Wilderness* by the Dutch artist. John-in-the-wilderness was there to confirm what the research says: that it is indeed hard to be alone with your thoughts when there is nothing around to distract you. The "Just Think" study discovered some unsurprising things about what happens when you take phones and even pencils away from Americans – no texting, no doodling – and ask them to spend some time alone thinking in an empty room: they do not like it. Regardless of whether the volunteer study participants (both university undergraduates and community members) were left to their own mental devices or were asked to think about prescribed topics (like going out to eat, or playing a sport) "about 50% of people did not like the experience, reporting an enjoyment level at or below the midpoint of the scale" in addition to giving generally "high ratings of boredom" (Whitehead 2014).

Whereas the AAAS interpretation of the study frames boredom as a function of the individual having nothing to do, I suggest that the boredom of the study would be better described in terms of overload and disaffect since it was the very choice of what to think about that contributed to the negative experience of the subjects. Again, this is not absence, this is *disaffection*. Without the benefit of a habitual mode of thought, like the prayerfulness of St John in the wilderness, the participants had no structure for their thinking that might make their boredom meaningful. In fact, the lead study author himself intends to pursue studies on meditation as a way to gain control over one's thoughts and make one's mind|body a more pleasant place to be, while also recognizing that meditative work is done within the context of a religious community. "As I say that," remarks Wilson (in Hutson 2014), "it sounds sort of audacious to say, well, the Buddhists have had two thousand years of mediation training, but I can train people to do it easier. We certainly haven't succeeded in doing it yet. This is something I want to test." Wilson's comment is narrativized in the AAAS story, which concludes that: "Because people so often find themselves intentionally or unintentionally wrapped up in their thoughts, the research team suggests that meditation or other techniques to relax and learn how to gain control of the mind could be helpful. If we knew how to steer our thoughts in a pleasant direction and enjoy the experience, maybe we wouldn't hate to be alone with ourselves." So what we see is that the popular discourse suggesting that the individual, unbound from matrices of interpersonal connection, has the power to "fix" the problem of boredom themselves. The popularizers move too quickly to resolve the boredom without theorizing its causes. This internalization of the responsibility for boredom obfuscates the overload context of ubiquitous digital information and communications technologies, ideological pluralism, proliferating consumer choice, and the disaffective experience of time accelerating and destabilizing basic cognitive processes. The emphasis on individual responsibility for boredom forgets the interpersonal matrix of networked connections and expectations.

Ultimately, what gets interpreted by science popularizers as an experiment on boredom is an attempt to recreate the conditions of an anachronistic nothing-to-do boredom artificial to twenty-first century conditions. While the study claims to empty the environment of stimulation and distraction (read: overload), leaving participants with nothing but their own thoughts, it cannot actually do so because the individual has already been disaffected by the overload boredom of the info-sphere. They are carrying the effects of the info-sphere with them. Their boundaries between self and the info-capitalist environment have already blurred. Participants entered into the study already habitualized to the disaffect of overload boredom – a boredom in which they are constantly asked to choose this, choose that, choose now. The study simply offered them more choice, to which the response was more boredom or more stimulation (the shock). The popularizers of this research inadvertently misrepresent what boredom is today by suggesting that boredom is about the understimulation of the individual. The piecemeal strategies they suggest for choosing your way out of boredom – like learning meditation, downloading productivity apps, and adopting time management strategies – are twentieth century approaches to solving twenty-first century overload.

More importantly, as mentioned above, these boredom-avoidance strategies actually feed back into overload boredom: they encourage the individual to collapse in on themselves by thinking only of their own individuality, their own mindfulness, their own interiority, cut off from their networked selves. However, because of the very nature of overload boredom, we cannot ignore the media ecology of the info-sphere, which acts as an ever-present outside constantly informing our interiority. Our twenty-first century digital wilderness is full of smartphones, laptops, tablets, and social media services, like digital-virtual demons of akēdia. And connecting ourselves to these devices in weak networks (see Stalder 2013; Castells 2004) results in our social relationships densifying online, even as this densification collapses real, live others into their two-dimensional avatars. These avatars of our relationships sit alongside an array of other media distractions that are infinite in number and always available. In this interconnected condition of possibility, the world becomes browsable, always "there," and therefore seems distant, and passive (see Mitchell 2014). Yet it is nevertheless making constant demands on our attention. But these are invisible demands. The more world that waits to be browsed, the more we must actively scroll through it. But in scrolling there is a stasis.

Your hand moves on the mouse and your fingers slide on the touch screen, moving but going nowhere, like a perceptual version of the "spinning wheel of death" on your computer screen (at least if you are an Apple user). This habitual, reflexive cycle scrambles our affective read on our interiority; by tying up our attentional resources it compromises our ability to actually know and feel ourselves from within. These disaffective consequences of overload boredom destabilize our relationships to others, both carbon and silicon, and even our very model of the world itself.

With this affect theory approach in hand we can begin to see how overload boredom is a crisis of meaning in the twenty-first century, but one that we can use to generate new meaning – indeed we already do this. We can make meaning out of overload boredom by attuning to a model of the world that reads the current state of our disrupted and disaffected interpersonal matrix within the fundamental conditions of our twenty-first century digital-technical reality. Such a model, for which I draw on the speculative realism of N. Katherine Hayles, Jane Bennett, and others, breaks us out of obsessive interiority by sensing the subject-object duality that is shared by selves and other beings.

We must pause here to ask: is there a way to account for the differences between subjects and objects (and the human and nonhuman figures who occupy these positions) under racial heteropatriarchal capitalism whilst also thinking about enchanting modes of overlapping human being and thinghood? As Levi Bryant (2013, 17) writes in "Politics and Speculative Realism":

> The apparently abstract concerns of SR have generated so much controversy in politically oriented domains of the humanities. Through its critique of correlationism and its defense of realism, SR risks arguing that the king really is a king. In other words, critiques of correlationism and defenses of realism are not mere technical philosophical issues, but have very significant political implications. Radical emancipatory political theory has been correlationist and anti-realist through and through. In arguing that it is language and social practices that carve up the world, CT is correlationist in that it treats categories or types as resulting from our discourse about the world. It is anti-realist in arguing that types or kinds that we attribute to the social world – "male," "female," "straight," "gay," "black," "white," and so on – are the result of social constructions, of discourses

> and practices, and are therefore not natural kinds. Seen in this light, blanket condemnations of correlationism risk undermining decades of hard-won emancipatory victories in the name of justice and equality.

What we can do if we want a political theory inflected by speculative realism yet sympathetic to critical theory is define what kind of critique is appropriate to different domains: what Bryant divides (via Lacan) into the real, the symbolic, and the imaginary. That is:

> The domain of the Symbolic would retain the claims of traditional [critical theory] and would constitute what we might call "semiopolitics" or the critical unmasking and debunking of discourses and narratives legitimizing various power relations and identities through appeals to nature, divine orders, and ahistorical essences. The domain of the Imaginary would be the domain of human and alien phenomenology, exploring the lived experience of how humans encounter the world about them, but also how various nonhumans such as animals, bacteria, plants, technologies, and institutions selectively relate to the world about them. Finally, the domain of the Real would be the exploration of those properties that really do belong to things and the efficacy things organize on other things. (Bryant 2013, 19–20)

In this way, speculative realist ontology can be consilient with empirical evidence, from physical realities, to sociological ones.

But how might speculative realism work as a methodology? "First, one needs a substantial body of knowledge, usually gained from scientific, technical, or engineering sources. Then one extrapolates into perceptions or world views, speculating about how that object encounters the world ... To exist in the world, every object that does so must have a certain internal coherence; otherwise, it could not endure for even a nanosecond ... Because of this coherence, it is possible to develop accounts that have causal and predictive efficacy. This does not mean, however, that such accounts have exhausted (or can ever exhaust) all of an object's way of being in the world" (Hayles 2014, 172). But the conditions of overload make it harder to develop this method of speculative inquiry. Information and choice overload take what was once a substantial body of knowledge up to the scale of the totality of globe-spanning inter-networked connections and archives. In this information super-infrastructure, each individual person moreover has access to the entirety of the collective information, which our affecognitive biology has not evolved to deal with. Because we are overloaded in this way, we cannot experience the internal coherence of objects, which means the task of speculating about them is made more difficult. This is an impossible task in the conditions set up by modern ontological conceptions of self and the boredom that self experiences. The shortcomings of this modern ontology are compounded by the overload of information and choice that militate against the integration of information about "the impersonal life that surrounds and infuses us" (Bennett 2010, 4). This overload disaffects our capacity for "subtle awareness of the complicated web of dissonant connections between bodies," thus rendering the task of speculative inquiry all the more necessary.

A SPECULATIVE REALIST INQUIRY INTO OVERLOAD BOREDOM

What is the task of speculative inquiry into overload boredom? Speculative inquiry, according to Hayles, requires an affective and aesthetic orientation that endeavours "to recognise that every real object possesses ... its own experience of the world" (2014, 178). This inquiry is "potently suited to a posthuman world in which other species, objects, and artificial intelligences compete and cooperate to fashion the dynamic environments in which we all live" (Hayles 2014, 179). To so inquire into overload boredom, we need to relativize the self by speculating on how the self is like the other objects in the world, and how objects in the world are more like selves than (modern, Western) common sense allows. We must imaginatively project ourselves "into other objects' experience of the world" (Hayles 2014, 177). Human beings are not so different from other creatures and agencies in the wilderness of things. While we might differ in terms of complexity or experience, we intersect, intensively, through networked connections and engagements of bodies, technologies, and society. All things have their own encounters in the world, but "humans as a species have developed ways to access far more perspectives than any other" beings (Hayles 2014, 171). I propose we take advantage of this.

But this is not as easy as it might first appear. Human beings differ from other bodies insofar as we have the capacity to know ourselves affectively from within, in relation to the without. But our privileged access *to ourselves*, our interiority, is notoriously limited. Most of our thoughts are unthought (Hayles 2017); we use cognitive processes that are inaccessible to consciousness yet necessary for it to function. Likewise, our access to the world is radically limited. We are only sensitive, for instance, to the information that comes from a certain colour spectrum, a certain decibel range, a certain set of macroscopic mid-size objects. These limitations are why we use technology to expand our sensorium. Unfortunately, we have made the mistake of thinking we can use the same technology to expand our access to our inward selves. As we open ourselves to the interface, we might perceive the encounter as singular: one technological object, and one piece of information displayed in it. But attached to the encounter is an overload of information, actively bearing down on us, hidden only by virtue of its size. This overload of information congests our interiority like afternoon traffic – or, in other words, we increase in affecognitive entropy – meaning that we lose capacity to speculate on ourselves. This in turn makes it harder to speculate on the interiority of other things.

We *can* expand the attentional capacity inside our brains to receive information arriving from the info-sphere (re: Berardi on being more productive in the field of attention) but in the end, this interior expansion mainly serves to dredge up more information to feed back into information technologies, which both deliver and demand information. The medium of overload boredom filters our world by selecting for volume and speed, the ingredients on which info-capitalist production depends. Our ability to comprehend how we process those materials is not helped by our information technologies, it is actively hampered by them. This is not to say that impulse to expand access to our inner selves is misguided, but rather that the concepts behind information technology are fundamentally unsuited for this purpose because they are based on the wrong ontology. They are based on the ontology of the Western liberal autonomous subject that sees human beings as essentially different and separate from every other kind of being, including our information technologies, and sees human beings as in control of them. As The Invisible Committee (2014) points out, info-capitalism gives rise to: "a being which, armed with its Apple Watch, comes to understand itself entirely on the basis of external data, the statistics that each of its behaviors generates. A Quantified Self that is willing to monitor, measure, and desperately optimize every one of its gestures and each of its affects (110) … Eventually, however, with Western man's [sic] abstract relation to the world becoming objectified in a whole complex of apparatuses, a whole universe of virtual reproductions, the path towards presence paradoxically reopens" (117). The technologies of info-capitalism do not help us get a better read on how information and affect arrives into our consciousness; instead, they overload our affective and cognitive processing capabilities. The Invisible Committee goes on to say "by detaching ourselves from everything, we'll end up detaching ourselves even from our detachment" (117). But the affective milieu of overload boredom makes it impossible to detach from our detachment because the very nature of the world is consistent and constant attachments between objects.

Speculative inquiry is what gives us hope for detaching from detachment, or at least moving through overload boredom in a way that coheres. "The hope," writes Bennett (2010, 4), is that speculative realist inquiry "will enhance receptivity to the impersonal life that surrounds and infuses us ... and will enable wiser interventions into that ecology." So in the context of overload boredom, instead of – or to counter – the misguided use of technology to access our inner selves, we need to devise speculative probes for capturing what usually passes beneath notice in ourselves. We need to experiment with the idea that our own inner lives are not so different from the inner lives of other things.

In order to cultivate this sensitivity, I draw from the speculative realism synthesized by both Bennett and Hayles. These thinkers advocate embracing aesthetic means as a way to enter into other objects. Rather than ask what is it like to be a bat (Nagel 1974), they ask "what is it like to be ... anything."[3] This is the basis of an *enchanted materialism* that emphasizes the agency of objects, or things, or other-than-human matter. An enchantment that refers to a "strange combination of delight and disturbance" (Bennett 2010, xi), and a "complex mood ... accompanied by a heightening of sensuous or aesthetic experience" (Bennett 2001, 37). This enchanted materialism explores the many, non-mechanical ways "things ... *produce* (helpful, harmful) effects in human and other bodies" (Bennett 2010, xii). It highlights "the extent to which human being and thinghood overlap. The extent to which the us and the it slip-slide into each other" (Bennett 2010, 4). If we do attune ourselves to such a model of the world, we can approach relations between humans and non-humans despite the fact that these relations are often not manifested in our own conscious experience on account of the affecognitive confusion of overload boredom. Indeed, it is the very fact that they withdraw from conscious experience that makes them so valuable for speculation.

Withdrawal

For certain strains of speculative realism, withdrawal is a fundamental relation between objects. Hence the oft-cited example of fire contacting cotton (Harman 2010b): what matters about cotton for fire is not its whiteness or softness, but its flammability. For fire, the rest of cotton withdraws. This example is intended to show that objects do not passively present their qualities, they meet what is relevant for each other, and in that meeting there is both contact and withdrawal (what qualities that do not manifest can be said to be withdrawn). Another famous example, Heidegger's "well wrought hammer," likewise illustrates that most of our contact with things is actually not through their being consciously present to us. If the hammer I am hammering with is "well wrought" then I do not notice it until it breaks or slips out of my hand mid-strike. I think an aesthetic-affective reading shows withdrawal to be the key experiential texture of overload. In aesthetic-affective terms, withdrawal is "a feature of relationality per se, and no longer just a sad deficit of mournful human experience" (Harman 2010a).

How this functions in overload boredom is that withdrawal is happening both from all other beings and objects in the world, and also *from ourselves*. The withdrawal from ourselves prevents self-conscious reflexivity because an interiority in some sense becomes impossible when we are always so suffused by information-technology. If we view our interior as a withdrawal from the world, overload boredom is a withdrawal from this withdrawal.

As a consequence, overload boredom dampens our ability to connect, cathect, and invest affectively, leaving this deficit feeling more real and permanent than it is; as we encounter the deluge of objects in info-capitalist overload culture, our selves withdraw and we do not even experience ourselves withdrawing. The consequences of double withdrawal are severe: it is why the old strategies for dealing with boredom ("techniques to relax") no longer function; it is why speculative reason, which typically only focuses on a single withdrawal, can only get us so far; and it becomes the disaffective medium itself, the space in which objects "meet," or rather, don't. In the blooming buzzing confusion of the raw materials of meaning, the world can no longer be so easily separated between subjects and objects, as the subject retreats from the subject, and objects retreat from objects. Indeed in the blooming buzzing confusion of the raw materials of meaning, the world can no longer be so easily separated between subjects and objects, as objects withdrawing from objects is all there is. We should therefore adjust our understanding of the world to sense an "information sublime," which Robert Pepperell describes as "awe at this boundless realm of information that earlier generations felt towards the extremities of the natural world" (Pepperell 2009, 384). This sublime acts as an aesthetic prod to help the subject of overload boredom sense the separateness of itself from this world, and its separateness from itself. It even points towards a cause: that shared and immanent meaning has been drained by modernity's disenchanting forces.

Again, this is not a call for nostalgia, or even a return to older forms of boredom: we must make ontological, existential meaning out of overload, or endure a crisis of the spirit. In response to all this withdrawal, I want to cultivate an affect of intimacy when imagining all of the strange objects, phenomena, and agencies in the world. And I want to remain open to the loneliness and melancholy of that experience, as well; we must attune ourselves to sensing overload boredom so as not to continue withdrawing from it, get distracted from distraction, anesthetized. The more objects we encounter, the more information we are presented, the more withdrawal. Hence more painful feelings of separateness. Overload, as we know, both creates more object encounters and dampens our ability to sense withdrawal and the resultant loneliness and melancholy. It is thus that overload boredom disaffects. Psychic pain spreads into every corner of awareness, as it is trying to get our attention – but in overload culture our attention is consumed. Intentional and attentional distraction try to keep this pain at bay. As shown in the AAAS story, we have many piecemeal self-regulation strategies, but it is also an incidental function of our twenty-first century digital world that we have ubiquitous access to information and ubiquitous social reachability. The study participants used physical pain of electric shocks to distract from attending to the pain. As David Foster Wallace (2011, 84) points out in the epigraph to this chapter, a low-level pain provides just enough stimulation to distract people from some other, deeper type of pain that is always there. I suggest that attentiveness to recurrent withdrawal, and the loneliness and melancholy that follows, is more productive than more distractions or administering ourselves bargain-basement shock therapy.

Boredom is a form of self-conscious mediation, but when overloaded, functions as a disaffective medium that obscures self-conscious reflexivity as we withdraw even from our own withdrawal. For the modern subject, boredom was a creative function of the will that forestalls experiential presence in the world (Haladyn 2015). But now, the self (which ironically is obsessed with interiority) has lost a sense of itself even as an object in the world.

In overload boredom the locus of agency has shifted so that it is not us but the medium of boredom that disaffects. Our technology use has shifted our agency out into the world and its objects, and the withdrawal/hit cycle forestalls the reflexive self-consciousness that it would take to fulfill the creative function of forestalling experiential presence. The condition of ubiquitous technology means that as the subject withdraws, omnipresent, of-the-moment online updates rush in. It is therefore less possible to reflect on the forestalling of experiential presence, and for it to be a self-conscious strategy.

CONCLUSION: APPROACHING OVERLOAD BOREDOM IN AN AESTHETIC-AFFECTIVE MODE

If theories of modern boredom see boredom as a response to mediation, my theory of twenty-first century boredom is a theory of boredom *as a disaffective medium* and cultural milieu: we are emptied of everything, even our emptiness, and become an overly full space of mediation between objects, themselves withdrawing. The "I" who is bored – the privileged, centred subject of our common sense psychology version of boredom – is no longer the proper topic of boredom. My speculative aesthetic-affective proposal is that we feel the loneliness and melancholy and generate intimacy in response to "alien" others, rather than withdrawal. Speculative realist ontology can help us approach overload boredom with the vulnerable affects of intimacy directed at ourselves as just a part of this world with its fundamental withdrawnness and unknownness, as well as its relationality and becoming. The aesthetic-affective plays a receptive, attuning role that thaws the anaesthetic, undoes the disaffect of overload boredom by seeing the subject and the object differently, yet not so different from each other. It is, of course, a partial, provisional, and speculative solution, but it affords a new approach to boredom as an existential concern, a spiritual crisis.

Now that we have unlimited connection to things, what we need is a new ethics of attending better to withdrawal. Becoming intimate with the pain of all the withdrawing objects of overload boredom frees us from the moral pressure of choosing how to most productively instrumentalize them in the service of info-capitalism. In the next chapters I mobilize this aesthetic-affective imagination in a series of case studies of art objects that take surplus information as their medium or message in order to negotiate the spiritual crisis of overload boredom in and through the resources of info-driven, hyperconnected, info-capitalist society. These include the seemingly obsessive practice of texting and social media use more broadly, as well as literary practices of conceptual writing that use digital strategies like generating text from search engine results or that thematically reflect on life in the information society.

3

Habritual Texting

Why We Are Addicted to Boring Conversation

I never seem to recognize important moments at the time they're going on – they always seem like distractions from what I'm really supposed to be doing.

David Foster Wallace, *The Pale King*

On the screen of an iPhone, a message appears containing only a stack of clock emojis, hands all arrayed at different times. And then another. Next, a message with the text "W8ING 4" and the emoji of a grey silhouette of a man. Then another stack of clocks, appearing so fast they must have been copy-and-pasted. Then the three dots that indicate someone is typing back. Now it seems if someone is typing "back," then all the symbols of time and impatience must have been coming from "our" side of the screen. This is not a record of a chat, it is a poem – Sophia Le Fraga's *W8ING* (2014). And this poem is in the form of a video. There is sound, but no voices. No one would be able to speak most of the abbreviations and symbols and emojis that show up on screen anyway. There are just the clipped *whoosh* sounds of the message sent/message alert tones. We see "our" side of the texts getting composed, but no hands tapping the keyboard. And not in real time, either, but faster than anyone could humanly type. "Our" side is called $OPH. $OPH's interlocutor has no name. The more these two characters talk, the more nothing happens. It is a cheeky way of showing what it is to hurry up and wait in the social space of digital chat. *W8ING* is a texting take on Samuel Beckett's boredom play *Waiting for Godot*. Le Fraga's poetic interpretation casts us as the protagonist, the iPhone user $OPH. $OPH types:

W8 / So yr back? //

The other side responds obtusely:

> Am I? //

A terse back-and-forth gets going:

> I was starting to think you were gone forever //
> Me 2 tho //
> we'll have to celebr8 / this being together at last //
> not now but l8tr def //
> lol //

It is not clear whether the two are properly understanding one another, or even really getting along. Like the play *W8ING* riffs on, it gets more absurd. $OPH and the unnamed character go back and forth suggesting they ought to leave the conversation and then reminding each other that they can't because they are waiting for the emoji-silhouette-of-a-man. Eventually the unnamed character – the "friend"? – observes:

> we don't rly ever stfu lol //
> It's so we don't think //
> I guess / living is like / not enough //
> We have 2 txt abt it //
> sooooooooooooo say something //
> Chill / I'm trying //

Then later, the friend says:

> We always find sumthin 2 do that makes us feel like we exist / amirite //

And finally, at the end:

> Do you think god sees me? //

$OPH replies:

> you gotta close your eyes //

More clocks close the poem off. In *w8ING* the two characters are shooting the shit, feeling compelled to remain in the conversation, toggling between boredom and interest, loneliness and communion, surface and depth, optimism and despair, antagonizing and comforting each other, killing time and looking to each other for meaningful stimulation. This digital disturbance of time and meaning by too much information and choice is the disaffective texture of overload boredom, and texting is one widespread, everyday practice in which this texture can be palpable. Its paradoxes are what I want to explore in this chapter.

DISTORTED TIME, ELUSIVE MEANING

The bored, impatient, laconic conversation pair in *w8ING* embody the worst of our relationships with our phones. At the same time, they show that there is nothing inherently less serious about working out our existential worries in them than in any other medium. Despite its cartoonish features, the fictional conversation takes existential anxiety seriously. The poem plays with the stereotype of disaffected kids obsessed with their phones by pairing youth slang with weird metaphysical moments suggesting the conversation partners are not so young ("all my life I've been like wtvr b reasonable like you haven't tried everything yet //"). The emotional tone of their interaction surfaces an awkward truth: that along with all the information our devices bring us comes an uncomfortable feeling that it is not making more sense.[1] There is too much of it, too fast and too fragmented, to integrate into long-lasting structures of shared meaning. Instead, the weight of the overload registers affecognitively in two fundamental ways that Le Fraga's poem illustrates: as a distortion of time and elusion of meaning (see figure 3.1).

The distortion of time is the sense of an off-tempo rhythm in the contemporary moment of media speed and ubiquity we inhabit; there is not only speed, there is also the flat-footed accent of delay. There is the actual time-lag of waiting for a reaction to something you have just typed, whereas in person you could glean much from the facial expression, body language, and little conversational sounds ("ah," "hm," "uhh") even while your conversation partner paused to gather their thoughts. There is the temporal drag of having to funnel your would-be speech and gestures through the bottleneck of "textspeak" (Crystal 2008, 80), emojis, GIFs, and other text-image hybrids.[2] There is the sense that, to the extent that digital interaction serves the

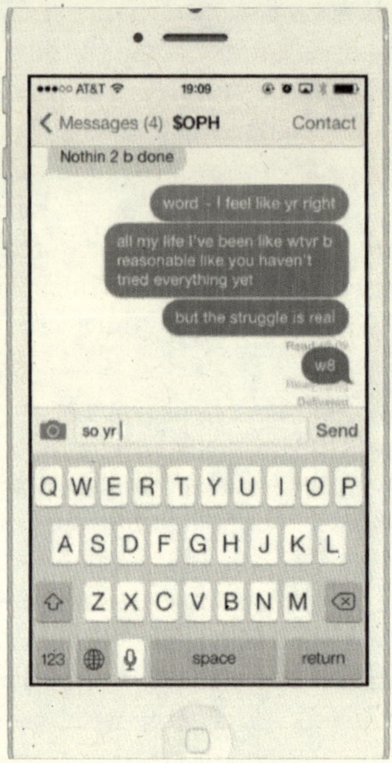

3.1 Screen capture of a video of Sophia Le Fraga's W8ING (2014). After the on-stage performance, Le Fraga did not publish the text of W8ING, except in a time-based form. Her website offers a link to a sped-up video of her phone sending and receiving the texts that comprise the piece. There, W8ING is grouped with two other digitally reimagined plays under the heading *The Anti-Plays (2014–15)*.

purpose of either planning for or substituting physical interaction, it holds you in a state of suspense before the "real action." As in the epigraph to this chapter, present moments seem like distractions from what is really supposed to be happening.

The elusion of meaning is in the "flattening" of a huge diversity of activities into the two-dimensional face of the digital screen. It is in the bubbling of our individual experiences that happen through those screens so that even as we are potentially more "connected" to those we wish to have in our networks, we may also have far less sense of what others are experiencing in their own bubbles. The writer Susan Dominus (2015) notes that in her own pre-Internet childhood: "All was overt: There was much shared experience and little uncertainty. Now, by contrast, among our closest friends and family members, we operate furtively without even trying to, for no reason other than that we are using a nearly omnipresent, highly convenient tool, the specific use of which is almost never apparent … My own children do not know when I am searching for a phone number, because all they see is me, on my iPhone, intently focused on something mysterious and decidedly not them ... someone slightly bored, distracting herself with some mindless electronic pursuit." The elusion of meaning is in distraction from distraction from distraction. It is in rarely having the opportunity to be bored in the "traditional" way (re: Benjamin). It is in using devices like the iPhone out of compulsion – because compulsion does not require foregoing one thing in order to commit to another, which is what would turn the haunting arbitrariness of choice into an act of valuation. The elusion of meaning is in the problem of recognizing, as T.S. Eliot (1934) asked in "The Rock": where is the wisdom lost in knowledge, and where is the knowledge lost in information?

THE LINK BETWEEN CHOICE OVERLOAD, INFORMATION OVERLOAD, AND OVERLOAD BOREDOM

Texting shows how a fundamental component of the information society can offer the existential goods of togetherness, commonness, and community and be inextricably tangled with the surfeit of choice and information that corresponds with the spiritual crisis of overload boredom. The always-open communication channel with a texting partner forever invites a response and never suggests a stopping point ("we don't rly ever stfu lol //"). Over time, being reachable by text takes on the character of a tacit mutual obligation that matches the way that social media broadly "enhance their reach," enabling "users to organize the world as a series of interesting (and eventually, ultimately, boring) distractions that are always available" (Mitchell 2014). Rich Ling and Jonathan Donner (2009, 29) call this "ubiquitous reachability"; the expectation is that if I am reachable, then so are you. Scale this up to as many contacts as you do or could have in your phone, and the volume of inbound information can easily crowd out other sources of information.

In addition to ubiquitous reachability, the number of choices about whom to write or write back, how much, and how often, is definitely larger than what is optimal for psychological and social wellbeing. It is a big cognitive job to evaluate more than a certain, modest set of choices.[3] The more choices you have, the more information you must gather, the more comparisons you must make, and the more opportunity cost (or "fear of missing out") you must endure. Etiquette and expectations in the digital frontier are indeterminate and this indeterminacy heightens points of negotiation and decision-making.

For example, responding quickly could mean that you spend your day responding frequently. You may be less lonely, but you will be more distracted and frantic. Responding slowly could mean that what is put out of sight is out of mind, and forgotten completely. You may be calmer, but lonelier. The accumulation of these choices is a source of hesitancy in the otherwise high-revving engine of social media. Just as the "action" in *W8ING* is both fast and slow, the overload pattern, the *temporality* of overload, involves boredom as the "lag in which the slow horse of meaning is unable to keep up with the fast horse of mere information" (Klapp 1991, 173). Many choices may be small on their own, but they become significant as part of a choice overload pattern.

"Making choices has become a very lonely act" amid "today's individualism," as the philosopher Renata Salecl says (2009, 177). With only the time, ability, and resources to pursue certain choices and not others, people have to shoulder the responsibility of being "some kind of self-creators" (Salecl 2006, 132). For these reasons, too much choice and information is demotivating. The state of disconnect between limited agency and apparently unlimited choices is characterised by a constant tension that Salecl (ibid., 134) shorthands as "the tyranny of choice" ("Ughhhhh / Wut do we do now? // girl lol idkkkkk // Lets gtfo asap // omg we legit can't //").

The illusion of unlimited choice is convincing because the late modern logic of choice has a way of masking its own workings. It does so by proffering the freedom to choose among supposedly limitless options without providing any real sense of *alternatives*. If my choices are not hooked up to social consequences or shared systems of meaning, they might therefore seem pointless. If my choices seem essentially interchangeable, they therefore might as well be random. The infinite substitutability of options is reinforced by the logic of substitutability in social systems: in the abstract equivalence of money; the "substitution of the circulation of things for human relations" (Legge 2016, 92); the similarity of form taken by both labour and leisure as they are channeled through the same devices. The pursuit of a succession of novelties becomes, itself, repetitious, as does waiting for the next input, the next tally of likes, retweets, followers, the next message. This is a collection that has no terminal object.

The more this temporality of searching and waiting reigns, the more it drains "the world of qualitative differences" (Gardiner 2016, 243), erodes a basic sense of voluntariness, condones a quiescence of personal and political will ("Nothin 2 b done // word – I feel like yr right //"). Scale the psychological choice and information overload up to the societal level and it follows that the cumulative effect can be one of jagged temporality and affecognitive withdrawal: an atmosphere of overload boredom.

THE TEMPORAL LEVERS OF TEXTING

Choice and information are two dimensions of the overload boredom problem, and texting offers some temporal levers for controlling them. When you choose to reach out and reply, or not, is always a matter of accelerating or decelerating interpersonal temporalities ("sooooooooooooo say something // Chill / I'm trying //"). Everyone knows that, unlike a posted letter, we usually *can* deliver a text response rapidly. (Even the verb "to text" or "to message," or some "verbing" of a specific app, connotes something different than the verb "to write" does; something permissibly fragmentary and spontaneous, or "something casual and inconspicuous, to deploy Heidegger's (1995) language of boredom" [Mitchell 2014]). But, unlike, say, the phone or the door, we often *don't* answer right away (see Bosker 2011). We may feel at leisure, perhaps even encouraged, to wait some time before responding to a text, because it does not necessarily have an end in the same way a phone conversation does ($OPH's conversation never precisely ends – it opens and closes with a visual of time passing and suggests that more or less the same conversation plays out daily). There is a "reflective side" of texting,[4] where the addictive aspects of social media co-exist alongside opportunities to linger on the carefully composed words of a correspondent and to precisely choose our own in reply. It is possible to elongate the perception of time by paying close attention[5] – to perform a sort of close reading. Moreover, the very possibility of receiving a whole expression at once depends upon the fact that the sender can *delay* responding until their message is fully composed (a few times, the typing bubbles of $OPH's interlocutor pop up and disappear again).

But just as there are ways in which the intrinsic timescale of texting can be used to manipulate temporality, there are ways in which it manipulates us. The technology itself drives a certain immediacy. Apps like iMessage persuasively suggest their own content by presenting a curated set of prefabricated options in the form of emojis and autocorrect suggestions (in *W8ING*, we see the misspelling "eurs" before it's corrected to "eyes"; we see the autocapitalization of "I" rejected in favour of the lowercase "i" which $OPH tacks on to form the phrase "iMean"). Texting also makes demands on time. Remembering to reply can be a chore. Repetitious small talk ("so this is chill // Super dope //") can be tedious. It is impoverished of sensory cues that could bring the 2D bits of type to life – the eye-crinkle of a true smile, the prosody of speech.

Schematised roughly, texting could be said to follow the back-and-forth form of reaching out with a message → affirming with a response → message → response, etc. In any pattern, along with repetition and difference, there is presence and absence. As Jean Baudrillard wrote, "it is usually not an object's presence but far more often its absence that clears the way for social intercourse" ([1968] 2005, 113). Why? Because, among other reasons, disappearance is the precondition for reappearance. We must experience the loss of an object in order to refresh our desire for it. Texting enables us to speed up and slow down the back-and-forth rhythm of exchange and to pause it entirely while savouring a crystallised moment in a pleasurable dynamic or ruminating over what the receiver will make of our reply. Participating is not just a kind of social obligation (whose etiquette is far from settled), but also a way of hastening, delaying, and suspending moments of connection through both the affordances and exigencies of the communicative rhythm. If boredom (psychologically) can be described as "the desire for desires,"[6] texting deals with it by sustaining a state of wanting. Or, more pessimistically, it moves the pendulum that swings "to and fro between" the "pain" of failing to achieve our will and the "boredom" of willing nothing at all once our will has been satisfied (Schopenhauer 1969 [1818], 312). These dynamics account, in part, for why staving off boredom with texting tends to reproduce some of the conditions that were boring in the first place – like interminable pauses of dead air, and exchanges of low-quality, trivial information about our days – and yet can be addictive. More importantly, however much these behaviours might ease subjective feelings of boredom in any given moment, they reproduce the disaffective conditions of overload boredom by keeping the variables of choice and information unpredictable and always on. As $OPH says: "the struggle is real //."

RITUAL, HABIT, ADDICTION: HABRITUAL TEXTING

Making a choice is an expression of will, but acting out of habit is making a choice we are no longer aware of making. Texting often slides into this compulsive, physical register, which makes it a target of derision for being timewasting (iPhone users send and receive around fifty-three messages per day, on average, worldwide [Burke 2018])[7] and lazy (a way "to avoid conflict, from making lying easier to dodging in-person confrontation ... a far cry from paying attention ... to the thoughts and feelings of another person" [Mulqueen 2019]). While texting is habitual, it is also ritual, in the sense of something done in a patterned way to affirm a bond. It is a ritual of producing and consuming information that serves as a source of solidarity and identification for the individuals involved (see Lofton 2017). Texting is both a habit that compels us and a ritual that makes meaning out of overload – a "habritual," as I will call it.

Everyday Ritual

Ritual situations, observed the sociologist Erving Goffman, "can be quite simple and fleeting" so long as "we mutually realize we are both entrained" in a shared situation and "a common mood" (Ling 2008, 18). Goffman (1967) famously theorized the minutiae of face-to-face behaviour in terms of "interaction ritual," which, like any ritual, may serve to stabilize subjectivity, inculcate dispositions and beliefs, transform relationships, cement group bonds, or manage the flow of time. Richard Schechner (1974), a founder of "performance studies," conceived of all kinds of social dramas as both entertaining (that is, "theatrical") and efficacious (that is, "ritual") performances. In the "ritual model of communication" developed by communication theorist James Carey, information itself is drama. Ritual communication is communication that is not transmissive of information, but is meaningful, because what the communication does is provide a framework and a template for sharing, participation, association, and fellowship. Carey understood that this kind of communication could be so meaningful that he chose to use the term "ritual" to describe it on account of the religious connotations of "ritual." For Carey, this connection to religion helps to emphasize the concept of shared beliefs and ceremony that are fundamental to the ritual view. The topic of ritual communication could therefore be the weather, how you are doing, or some other garden variety thing. But the context makes it meaningful. It takes something that, in other circumstances would be small talk, and turns it into something of spiritual significance.

But what *is* that transformative context? In a word: shared. The kind of context that would transform boring small talk into ritual communication is one where the parties can feel like it represents and reinforces an underlying order of things in a social world they each inhabit. "Shared information circulating in an organic system" (Carey 1992, 23) is the binding force that makes culture possible and makes social processes possible. Communication functions ritually when it manifests these processes. But it functions less this way the less our social worlds actually overlap with one another. Here again, information overload and choice overload show up together: so much entertainment, news, and other content is generated every second of every day that the paths we choose through it will necessarily be so different that two neighbours or office mates or school friends might never have heard of the media each other knows best. There is a fragmentation of culture on this micro level of personal reference points, as well as at the level of subcultures associated with particular forms of lifestyle, values, or commodification.[8] It even happens within text conversations that a shared sense of purpose and tone gets lost.

There is a sketch by the comedy duo Key and Peele called "Text Message Confusion" (2018) that makes fun of what happens when friends misunderstand the tone of each other's text messages while trying to make plans. The two actors are playing themselves in this bit, and the premise is that they are trying to find a time to hang out. Michael-Keegan Key's character is trying to get in touch with Jordan Peele's character, who is happily occupied playing a video game and hadn't noticed his messages for a few hours.

"I've been trying to reach out to you all day. Are we on for tonight?" Peele's character does not clue into the frustration in Key's messages and sends a series of quick casual messages in response.

"Sorry dude. Missed your texts. I assumed we'd meet at the bar. Whatever. I don't care."

Key reads his friend's messages as blowing him off. Key reads the rest of Peele's messages with the same mounting rage he's experiencing, ignorant of the bland tone with which Peele is reading aloud the messages he is receiving and sending. The men eventually show up at the bar where they had made plans to meet, Peele holding drinks for his friend, and Key holding a baseball bat with a nail in it. With his assumption still that nothing is out of the ordinary, Peele takes the baseball bat to be a gift. Chuffed, he says:

"For my post-apocalyptic Jackie Robinson costume – how did you *know*?"

Peele's attitude in the text conversation is totally banal. He appears bored, but in a relaxed way. He is occupied by his video game, and he is not distressed by the low-level, perfunctory conversation because they are making plans. The communication is just about the transmission of information for a planning purpose. Key, on the other hand, is upset because he has not been able to read his friend's emotional tone, and vice versa.

This bit is great because it highlights a huge problem with texting: context. Establishing shared context in this exchange of information has two important dimensions: the purpose of the texting and the emotional tone of it. Texting makes it possible to leave these contextual dimensions unspecified to a greater degree than modes that provide a richer set of sensory cues about what is going on and why. Texting is a medium of communication that can bridge a gap between people, but when texting is preferred to other ways of communicating, choosing text can also be a way of choosing to hold this gap open, and hold the other at bay.

Even when ritual communication in Carey's sense fails in texting, we can still consider the "low-level" interaction of asynchronous communication in ritual terms. The formulaic, repetitive action in the case of texting is the spontaneous composition of short, typed notes. These messages transmit information, but also constitute an ongoing and co-present interaction. With the smartphone screen playing the role of mirror, this involves representing "the self to the self" as much as it does performing the self to others through "symbolic inter-personal communication" (Katz 2003, 315–18). Texting "enables shared ritual, retention of relationships, and the possibility to re-encounter experiences" (Wasserman 2011, 12). In this sense, "multiple parties' realisation of shared experience" through the exchange of little digital artefacts is the very basis of ritual. This is possible in part because the content of these messages is secondary to the fact of messaging (cf. Licoppe 2004). The expectation that there *will* be a return message clearly has a power having to do with the anticipation of a message even apart from its content ("ummm / please say like legit anything //"). Being targeted to personal contacts, texting is often not about "news," and the answer to "what's new" is just as likely to be some variant of "not much" as it is any substantive disclosure. The importance of messaging is precisely in establishing "connected presence" – that is, "the feeling of a permanent connection, an impression that the link can be activated at any time and that one can thus experience the other's engagement in the relationship at any time" (Licoppe 2004, 141). The ritual involves lighting up the circuit, no matter how brief the flicker.

If ritual conjures only the warmth of communion or orderly processing, it should not; amid the antiphony of message alert tones the "common mood" is about as likely to be one of anxious or bored waiting as it is likely to be the amity connoted by words like "connectivity" and "sharing" so often used to describe the digital social world ("Yesterday evening we were txting bout nothing in partic / That's been going on 4 like half a century now //"). Nonetheless, anticipation is the powerful negative of the same pattern in which reply is the positive. Even as we reach out to others, we put ourselves in the position of having to wait – for something, or maybe nothing, waiting for Godot.

Waiting

W8ING dramatizes how cycles of waiting, anticipation, disappointment unfold. Le Fraga tortures her audience a little bit by including the "typing bubbles" in her poem every time $OPH's interlocutor responds. These bubbles are a feature that is technically called the "typing awareness indicator." The typing awareness indicator used in some SMS[9] software and other apps is an ellipsis that appears on your screen while your interlocutor is entering characters, so that you know, according to creator David Auerbach (2014), "whether they [are] typing some huge message or … waiting for you to say something." This is essentially a cue for turn-taking in asynchronous communication, or, more accurately, "latent full-duplex" communication, which is when two parties can speak or write simultaneously but the transmission of the message is delayed until one or the other chooses to send it. In face-to-face communication there are breath cues, cooperative or competitive overlap, and all manner of body language and vocal intonation that manage transfer of speakership. It is fitting, then, to note that at one point it was estimated that "something like 95 percent of all message traffic through [MSN] Messenger servers consisted of those typing messages. Only 5 percent of messages actually contained *what users actually had typed*" (Auerbach 2014, italics in original). *W8ING* visualizes this aspect of the experience as part of its poetics. Just as we see the typing bubbles on the lefthand side of the screen, we also see $OPH correcting her typos as she goes. For $OPH and her interlocutor, sending and receiving messages is about transcending psychic isolation through co-presence, but also about creating a sense of anticipation about doing so, thus establishing some expectation about the structure of future time ("👤 should b here // he didn't say he'd for sure come tho // And if he doesn't come… // ? / we'll come back tmrw //").

But the typing indicator often "builds up the anticipation for a profound response only to disappoint you with the inevitable banality of what your friend actually says" (Auerbach 2014) ("Okay I'm tired // ugh //"). Auerbach (2014) says that for him as a user, "if there's any unease associated with the typing indicator, it's not from the added immediacy … but a lack of *enough* immediacy. It tells you that *something* is going on, but leaves you to wonder what it is." The fact that Le Fraga speeds up the video of *W8ING* to play back the conversation far faster than it originally occurred suggests she shares Auerbach's pain.

In fact, the typing awareness indicator has induced such widespread anxiety as to have spawned a published discourse. It began with the *New Republic* story editor Ben Crair's article "I Can See You Typing: The Most Awkward Part of Online Chat," in January 2014. In response, Auerbach issued an anti-apology in *Slate* the next month, "I Built That 'So-And-So-Is-Typing' Feature in Chat. And I'm Not Sorry." Several months later, the *New York Times* published a story by Jessica Bennett (2014) called "Bubbles Carry a Lot of Weight: Texting Anxiety Caused by Little Bubbles," which explored "modern-day technological minutiae that ha[ve] the ability to jail [users] in a very specific cognitive hell" ("we will w8 4 👤 // Ugh 😱 // omg this is the WORST / #HELP 🆘🆘🆘🆘 //"). It picked up on the previous two essays plus a story on *Medium* by the writer Maryam Abolfazli (2014) about the use of texting techniques to set expectations in romantic relationships without ever having to negotiate them directly ("Are We Dating? And Other Confusions Created by Texting"). By autumn these were followed by stories in *Boston.com* "Text Anxiety is Ruining Our Lives" (Raczka 2014) and *Elite Daily* "The Mid-Typing Texting Bubble is Actually Causing People Severe Anxiety" (Arata 2014).

Much of *W8ING* is watching these bubbles transform into words, putting a fine point on the fact that no matter how fast and frequently we type, it will only create a proportionate amount of waiting. The trouble with the bubbles has to do with the fact that, as already discussed, presence is not just expected on mobile devices, as Bennett (2014) says, "it's mandatory." The timescale of the message-response pattern between interlocutors can begin to collapse easily, and wedging it open most likely means that the gap is filled with dead air. The distress of these intermissions can be proportionate to the reward of reading and replying. "The typing indicator has become a message in and of itself, the equivalent of saying, 'Hold on, I'm responding' … Or … 'I'm not responding'" (Bennett 2014). This at least is confirmation of engagement with your message, which may offer some relief if your device has relayed the "read receipt" to indicate that the recipient has indeed received and opened it, but not yet replied. Bennett quotes informatics researcher Paul Dourish: "The awareness indicator … conveys that something is being done, but it won't say what. It's curiously coy." Abolfazli (2014) agrees: "The three dots shown while someone is drafting a message … is quite possibly the most important source of eternal hope and ultimate letdown in our daily lives. It's the modern-day version of watching paint dry, except you might be broken up with by the time the dots deliver" But as $OPH asks, "wd you rather be stuck doing nothing tho //"?

In trying to hurry along the arrow of time or at least loose it into the heart of some desideratum, Auerbach (2014) mimics Le Fraga's playwright poetics:

> Chatting and text messaging these days seems to combine the worst of both worlds, giving you just enough time in between messages to get bored without being able to do anything productive.
> Sometimes I miss the old days.
> So I'll sometimes
> insert extra line breaks
> in messages
> in the hopes of
> speeding up conversation
> or maintaining interest.

Auerbach's example is neither about establishing a relationship of unilateral control nor only about establishing an atmosphere of togetherness. It is also not just about transmitting information, either. It is ritual communication, in that it is directed less toward the extension of messages in space and more toward the maintenance of relation in time. If we think of texting as ritual performance, then we also see that the repetitive nature of this ongoing interaction bridges the past, present, and future by calibrating diurnal cycles, marking significant events or just establishing regular intervals within quotidian minutiae ("ugghhh wtf r we gonna do?!? // iMean there's nothing we can rly do // We're not too bad off, u & me // yaya🙌 //").

Repetition

As in all conversation, texting must navigate "two simultaneously functioning aspects overarching human communication, namely the presence of convention on the one hand, and the striving for individuality and idiosyncrasy on the other hand" (Urbanová 2007, 36). It must do so repetitively, however, in order to establish and maintain social contact between the participants in communication. In this sense, meaning can come from repetition, rather than difference, since it is the consistency of communication that shores up the interpersonal relationships carried out through texting. In ritual communication, we must therefore consider how the information *feels* – that is, how the circulation of information builds structures of knowledge, belief, and disbelief on our "landscapes of feeling" (Schaefer 2018, 70). We must imagine the reader or writer of texts less as a "sovereign, studious mind" and more "as a body enthralled, a body possessed, an addict" (69). A turning point in *W8ING* when the first ten minutes of going back and forth about whom they are waiting for, where, and why is interrupted by $OPH's interlocutor suggesting:

> I guess let's try to have a conversation / Since we apparently can't stop txting each other //

$OPH agrees:

> word / we don't rly ever stfu lol //

It is not that the pair cannot pull themselves away from an enthralling *conversation*, it is that they cannot stop the behaviour of texting *in spite of* the boring conversation.

The addictive frequency with which texting must be renewed means that even as it "breeds expertise" in using messaging technology for a variety of social ends, "it breeds boredom" (Chun 2014). In Chun's (2016) phrasing, this is a matter of "updating to remain the same" ("we'll come back tmrw // And then the day after tomorrow //"). To do this is to court a kind of stasis that promises social security but also threatens paralysis by forming a tenacious habit: "even as we become habituated to, and inhabitants of new media, new media … seeks to undermine the habits it also establishes … in order to be successful, in order to be new" (Chun 2014). But if we think of social media in terms of ritual communication, then we can appreciate how close "habit" and "ritual" are in conceptual proximity. Habits "bring out the creative in the machinic, the machinic in the creative. They embed the bodily in society, society in the bodily. Like a nun's habit, they mark an outer that's also an inner, that everyone can wear" (Chun 2014). The monastic metaphor is more than incidental; it is what is meant by the phrase "to do something religiously."[10] This is the nature of ritual. It is a powerful kind of compulsion that grows from the "the promiscuous cross-fertilization between the cognitive, the affective, and the religious" (Schaefer 2018, 81). Neurologically speaking, habits are behaviours that have moved from the associative to the sensorimotor loop. As "the vestiges of goals pursued," says Chun (2014), they are things that started as conscious, goal-directed behaviour, and have since flipped over to the domain of automatic behaviour ("so we weren't here yesterday evening / but what did we do then?? // DO?!! // idk like try & remember // Hmmm do … / Honestly / We were prob just txting //"). Considered in this light, the behaviours of checking the phone and tapping out a message really appear to be as much habit as ritual, and perhaps ritual as much in the sense of social maintenance as in addiction symptomatology.

Addiction

The word "addiction" co-occurs frequently with "social media."[11] A Google search of "texting addiction" yields pages of headlines from the past few years from the likes of *Forbes*, *Psychology Today*, CBS *News*, *Huffington Post*, *Daily Mail*, *Globe and Mail*, and a host of teen-specific websites. "Addiction" to texting is most often explained with the concept of "intermittent reward," introduced by behavioural psychologists Charles Ferster and B.F. Skinner in the 1950s. Not every time you check your phone will you find a message waiting for you, but sometimes you will. You receive the "reward" (the text message) only part of the time you perform the behaviour (checking your phone). And since you won't necessarily know when, there is incentive to keep checking. Addiction, in this sense, can be thought of as habit dysregulated by the temporality inherent to the texting medium itself ("Do you // do you / OMG jinx // Go ahead // no no you go first // Naaaa after u // no but I interrupted you tho //"). Many social networking technologies other than texting,[12] however, are deliberately designed to capitalise on this "powerful cognitive quirk," which compels us to repeat a behaviour over and over (Eyal 2012). They are what Nir Eyal calls "desire engines," keeping us enthralled by using an intermittent reinforcement schedule that induces that "semi-stressful response that we call desire." "Bizarrely," he says, "we perceive this trance-like state as fun ... because our brains are wired to search endlessly for the next reward, never satisfied" (Eyal 2012). Near the end of *W8ING* $OPH's interlocutor says:

> I'm tired //
> we're not in shape 💪 / how about a little deep breathing //
> I'm tired of breathing 😤 //

Irony sets the existential grievance at the heart of this quip at a distance beyond serious attention. $OPH passes it off coolly:

> word / yr right //

But in the next exchange, the final lines of the poem, the pair's metaphysical concerns become explicit:

> Do you think god sees me? //
> You gotta close yr eyes //

In the end *W8ING* suggests taking the enthralled body out of the stream of information, either making it or taking it in. Making oneself available to "god," to the world, "requires, the work seems to say, the end of *texting*, of making texts ... A new antinomianism?" (Weiner 2014). A counter to the fact that "our dopamine system works not to provide us with rewards for our efforts, but to keep us searching" (Eyal 2012). And waiting.

Habritual

Texting, with its socially binding functions and its compulsive bodily aspects, truly blends many senses of both habit and ritual such that the blend-word "habritual" captures its rote biomechanical and psychosocially meaningful aspects. This concept summarises a framework that suggests a very different way of thinking about a behaviour that is typically treated like a highly contagious social tic. It simultaneously emphasizes elements of nonhuman agency (e.g., social media as "desire engines") and the affective dimensions of the supposedly affect-neutral domain of information, and how they are linked in "affecognitive circuits" (Hamner 2018). Affecognitive circuits refer to "bodily, institutional, and personally and technologically mediated circuits of both felt response and thought response" (Hamner 2018). Through affecognitive circuits, "socially-distributed affects can harden into psycho-physiological habits" (Hamner 2018). Affecognitive states of boredom map onto the intersubjective unfolding of difference and repetition in the habits and rituals we play out in our social media technologies. These are what $OPH and her interlocutor illustrate as they banter about waiting for the unnamed person and try to provoke each other into providing some entertainment. And these habrituals are also "ontologically complex forces (affective and cognitive) of self-production" through which "publicness" eventually coalesces (Hamner 2018). This is what *W8ING* as a whole illustrates: how habritual texting reorganizes the technological, discursive, and affective conditions of ontology.

Texting is a granular site of experience within the conditions of overload boredom. Looking at texting as a habritual process shows how it creatively manipulates the variables of temporal and socio-emotional proximity. That is, when the object of our attention withdraws (when our interlocutor delivers nothing but maybe dots), we withdraw from the discomfort that creates within our own interiority by turning our focus outward. We summon the withdrawn object with a packet of information (a message) we produce as a lure. Yet, even as we may soothe our own psychological state of boredom with these actions, we also contribute to the conditions of overload boredom by maintaining ubiquitous reachability, and, therefore, maintaining a habritual of generating and consuming information through digital devices we tend to keep near us at all times.

CONCLUSION: COLLECTING, ARCHIVING, SHATTERING

We may sneer at it, but nobody who texts actually finds it insignificant; on the contrary, it is charged with the desire for discharging the burden of late modern digital selfhood. For many, texting holds the hope of closing the lonely gap between this self and an other. The medium is one of the most personal interfaces between self and overloaded digital world. There are three texting techniques in particular that bear considering: 1) deferring endings; 2) archiving the ephemeral; 3) transcending the self.

1 You Can Never Have Too Many Friends

When we send messages, we become charged with the potential of reply, which, discharged, may yield the return of a little semiotic gift, engendering some kind of reciprocity. Its unknown contents are curiosity-provoking. Sometimes, of course, the reply is disappointing and so we let our own response lapse so long that any conversation that picks back up is a new one ("🙏thnx god🙏 / I was starting to think you were gone forever //"). If we bother to pick it back up at all, it may likewise be about a kind of curiosity piqued by the way "constant updates prime us to fear we're missing out" (Bennett 2014). Or else we forget entirely and our forgetting restarts the cycle. It is like Baudrillard said of the collector; the pleasure is in dwelling in next-to-lastness. As long and insofar as the collection is never complete, the collector's subjecthood itself is felt to be without end. We might be burdened by the opportunity cost of knowing that untapped social connections are out there languishing somewhere, but perhaps we sometimes turn away from our proximate social prospects not in order to pursue these connections in and of themselves but in order not to exhaust the ones in front of us. Neither $OPH nor her interlocutor ever insist on getting to the bottom of whether their waiting is in vain, or admitting that maybe they set it up that way. The project of self-making is not only endless in the sense that choices never stop coming but also in the sense that connection and perpetually deferred closure is what symbolically transcends the finitude of the subject.

2 *The Archived Self*

As Baudrillard saw it, collecting affords "the possibility, from the present moment onwards, of continually experiencing the unfolding of [our] existence in a controlled, cyclical mode, symbolically transcending a real existence the irreversibility of whose progression [we are] powerless to affect" ([1968] 2005, 104). The peculiar digital materiality of the text makes it susceptible to being so collected in a way that speech acts are not, as *W8ING* illustrates, being a video poem full of language that cannot be spoken. The collection is also an archive; indeed, many devices specifically have a function called "archive," which stores old messages. In this way, digital "presencing" accumulates a history and sediments a legitimising past. It is a new way to fulfil an old psychological need, which Derrida (1995, 91) described like this: "To be *en mal d'archive* ... is never to rest, interminably, from searching for the archive right where it slips away ... it is to have a compulsive, repetitive, and nostalgic desire for the archive, an irrepressible desire to return to the origin, a homesickness, a nostalgia for the return to the most archaic place of absolute commencement." $OPH and friend play this desire out over and over, trying to locate themselves in what they perceive as a lack of place, a mysterious origin – a "void":

> We literally weren't here yesterday //
> W8 r u kidding where do you think we were then //
> How would I know? / In another compartment / There's no lack of void. //

The text archive secures a place to return just as the collection secures a place to go – a digital archive waiting to be browsed, where the subject is held "in a state of temporal abeyance" (Mitchell 2014), waiting.[13]

3 *Self-Shattering*

While the compulsion of text messaging can be explained in terms of self-making, it can also be thought of in terms of self-shattering, or a temporary release from a constraining individualism. Perhaps this is the sense in which $OPH's interlocutor claims to be tired of breathing; she is tired of performing her constant digital presence. The concept of self-shattering has roots in Sigmund Freud's ([1920; 1930] 1995) formulation of the "death drive."[14] Volker Woltersdorff (2012, 134) summarizes neatly: "The law of increasing entropy is a concept of energy in the natural sciences that assumes the tendency of all systems to eventually reach their lowest level of energy. Organic systems therefore tend toward inertia ... Since Freud identifies the death drive with entropy, within his theory, the economy of the death drive is to release tension." Therefore, the death drive surfaces widely beyond violent conflict,[15] including in the "time-stilled space-slowed" (Anderson 2004) state of boredom. (The Internet troll as bored, isolated malcontent is well established as a cultural trope and borne out by empirical data [Sanghani 2013; Mitchell 2013]).[16] But practices of "losing sight of self, evacuating value of selfhood" (Blas 2016) can be recuperated into practices of nonviolence – this is the principal sense in which self-shattering differs from the death drive. What it introduces is the idea that *in relationship* the assemblages of shattered selves might survive their being undone (Woltersdorff 2012, 148). To reach out through digital communication is not only to reach specific people, though it is that, too ("we'll have to celebr8/ this being together at last 🍻 //"). In a wider sense, it is to cast the net of attention in the hopes that it catches something, or rather, that something snags *it* among the overload of information. The moment of interest – a moment counter to boredom – is one of absorption. Connectivity, or co-presence, can be understood in this sense as a longing to obliterate our separate selves. We might imagine that if it were to be spoken aloud, there would be a stress on the "we" in $OPH and her friend's lines:

> We always find sumthin 2 do that makes us feel like we exist ... /
> amirite //
> ya lol 🎩 we're magicians //

It *is* a magic act to withdraw from the modern world and its "daily shocks" (Buck-Morss 1992, 16), only to reappear inside modern technologies to try to achieve moments of self-transcendence.

* * *

We may sneer at it, but nobody who texts actually finds it insignificant; on the contrary, it is charged with the desire for discharging the burden of late modern digital selfhood. The crisis of meaning in info-capitalist culture is not one of only vapid disengagement, but one of confronting choice and information overload through the enabling constraints of social media technologies. Though this cultural moment is *overloaded* its temporality is not universally fast, nor is all experience correspondingly shallow. The ambivalence of rejecting and also reproducing (psychological and overload) boredom through texting is a habitual technique of stabilizing the instability of spiritual crisis. Texting offers certain temporal levers for seeking stability amid a world of conflicting time-scales arising from the human, the digital, and the natural worlds jostling, interpenetrating one another, and vying for our attention.

There are other ways of generating personal information to seek being-in-common in social conditions characterized by overload. This is what I pursue in the next chapter. By further developing my theory of overload boredom in relation to information theory, I will show how sharing personal information is another way of co-presencing; it is a sharing of uncertainty, the effect of which is to revive some of the existential vulnerability and intimacy lost in the spiritual crisis of overload boredom.

4

Uncertainty and Shared Entropy in Overload Culture

We are all of us self-inaccessible and can, for example, touch parts of one another in ways that we could not even dream of with our own bodies.

David Foster Wallace, *Infinite Jest*

Open *i feel better after i type to you* to any page and you will see a string of text like this:

2006-05-09 02:15:41 go to bed
2006-05-09 02:16:16 if i work hard i don't think off
2006-05-09 02:17:29 left my computer down
2006-05-09 02:17:59 work hard
2006-05-09 02:19:11 get some sleep
2006-05-09 02:19:44 work tommorr
2006-05-09 02:20:44 bless night
2006-05-09 02:21:20 to tired to look at my clothes
2006-05-09 02:21:51 i was to tired to look at my clothes
2006-05-09 02:22:42 i have no one as song say
2006-05-09 02:23:12 have noone
2006-05-09 02:23:56 one warning
2006-05-09 02:25:07 if you ever fi nd someone never go though that process
2006-05-09 02:26:39 i tell the truth
2006-05-09 02:27:11 its to long
2006-05-09 02:27:46 will lose love
(AOL user 23187425 and Claburn 2006, 28–9)

Indicated by the dates on the string of search queries, the poem covers twenty-four days, for 254 pages. While the genre of writing is unclear, these curious, halting, time-stamped text fragments, like Le Fraga's *w8ING*, are a poem. Unlike *w8ING*, they are not text messages. They are a seemingly random assortment of web searches. And unlike *w8ING*, they are not a fiction of the artist's imagination. They are real, they are human, and they belong to AOL user 23187425. Yet, in this vast ream of entries, only a few of the searches yielded a result URL. So what was user 23187425 really searching for? What motivation propelled them through the tedium of typing into the void for so long? And how and why did thousands of their searches wind up published by the writer and coder Thomas Claburn?[1] And, more importantly, what can *i feel better after i type to you* tell us about boredom and meaning in a culture of overload?

As the story goes, in 2006 the company AOL accidentally released about 20 million search records from 650,000 users (Arrington 2006). The data includes all searches from those users for a three-month period that year, as well as whether they clicked on a result, what that result was and where it appeared on the result page. While the AOL username has been changed to a random ID number, the data includes highly sensitive information like personal names, addresses, social security numbers, and everything else someone might type into a search box. With all of those details, it would not be hard to identify individual users and what they were getting up to online. Technology columnists began publishing excerpts from various users that appeared to show bio sketches and to-do lists of truly astonishing turpitude. But the artist Thomas Claburn, who "writes text for people and code for machines" (according to his blog Lot49), saw some literary hybrid of the two in the millions of lines of search results. As a poem, *i feel better after i type to you* is an example of what's known as "antiexpressive" or "uncreative" aesthetics, "fusing the avant-garde impulses of the last century with the technologies of the present" (Goldsmith 2008).[2] Namely, antiexpressive art uses self-imposed constraints on choice to navigate huge swaths of information.[3] The point with such work:

> is not that anyone could do these works – of course they could – but rather that no one else has ... [Such] writing shows up the rhetorical, ideological force of our cultural sense of creativity, which clings so tenaciously to a gold standard of one's own words rather than to one's own idea or the integrity of that idea's execution. The hundred-thousandth lyric published this decade in which a plainspoken persona realizes a small profundity about

> suburban bourgeois life ... is somehow still within the bounds of the properly creative ... yet the first ... work to use previously written source texts in a novel way are still felt to be troublingly improper. (Dworkin 2011, xxxix)

This mode of writing seeks to mediate an encounter with an overwhelming dump of raw, unprocessed data, aestheticizing what would otherwise be a boring ream of text by engaging it under the terms normally reserved for creative writing.

Scrolling through the AOL data file, Claburn's attention was caught by the numerous, frequent, and poignant searches of user 23187425. Instead of evidencing a pattern of private interests and opinions, the search history revealed what Claburn recognized as a "poem of sorts" in the file (in Dworkin and Goldsmith 2011, 138). He collected it and formatted it lightly, adding page breaks and time headings between the user's apparent sessions, and gave it a title, which comes from a series of search queries at 1 AM, Friday 12 May:

> 2006-05-12 01:01:13 yellow notice for cable
> 2006-05-12 01:01:37 joe did
> 2006-05-12 01:02:22 want miss tv
> 2006-05-12 01:03:22 had it put on basic cable
> 2006-05-12 01:04:06 did watch tv a lot
> 2006-05-12 01:05:23 wal-mart 13" for 59.00
> 2006-05-12 01:06:33 i look at everything
> 2006-05-12 01:07:34 isle of black and white
> 2006-05-12 01:08:33 nice patio pillows
> 2006-05-12 01:09:11 not rain proof
> 2006-05-12 01:10:08 mean yes
> 2006-05-12 01:10:57 fit in my chairs
> 2006-05-12 01:11:34 go back over
> 2006-05-12 01:13:03 lowes has some red setting
> 2006-05-12 01:13:38 looking for four
> 2006-05-12 01:14:09 be here for life
> 2006-05-12 01:15:25 feel better after i type to you
> 2006-05-12 01:16:01 i feel better after i type to you
> 2006-05-12 01:16:44 joe blue line
> 2006-05-12 01:17:33 thank you
> (AOL user 23187425 and Claburn 2006, 69)

2006-05-09 01:59:49 music will not help me work
2006-05-09 02:00:24 take hands
2006-05-09 02:00:56 together
2006-05-09 02:01:47 my suit come tommorrow
2006-05-09 02:02:25 purse that match was gone
2006-05-09 02:03:40 say no
2006-05-09 02:04:11 altogether
2006-05-09 02:05:43 last two years white
2006-05-09 02:07:24 flower gold 2yrs ago
2006-05-09 02:08:06 gold flower 2 yrs ago
2006-05-09 02:08:33 white before that
2006-05-09 02:09:01 a pattern
2006-05-09 02:10:02 look that way
2006-05-09 02:10:49 gold suit picture turn backward
2006-05-09 02:11:40 the goldsuit picture turn backward
2006-05-09 02:12:53 all my picture
2006-05-09 02:13:51 frame broke high school picture
2006-05-09 02:14:43 out of all mine
2006-05-09 02:15:41 go to bed
2006-05-09 02:16:16 if i work hard i don't think off
2006-05-09 02:17:29 left my computer down
2006-05-09 02:17:59 work hard
2006-05-09 02:19:11 get some sleep
2006-05-09 02:19:44 work tommorr
2006-05-09 02:20:44 bless night
2006-05-09 02:21:20 to tired to look at my clothes
2006-05-09 02:21:51 i was to tired to look at my clothes
2006-05-09 02:22:42 i have no one as song say
2006-05-09 02:23:12 have noone
2006-05-09 02:23:56 one warning
2006-05-09 02:25:07 if you ever find someone never go though that process
2006-05-09 02:26:39 i tell the truth
2006-05-09 02:27:11 its to long
2006-05-09 02:27:46 will lose love
2006-05-09 02:29:25 that for a women with maids gardener and all
2006-05-09 02:29:50 laughing
2006-05-09 02:30:24 bought my own
2006-05-09 02:31:11 not a poor woman
2006-05-09 02:31:52 i have to work
2006-05-09 02:32:19 i have to work
2006-05-09 02:32:56 no dates no fun
2006-05-09 02:34:10 ready for bed
2006-05-09 02:34:37 not across

Tuesday 1:25 am

2006-05-09 01:25:15 break in
2006-05-09 01:26:00 joseph i have a question
2006-05-09 01:27:27 all the years why did you work out of delphi
2006-05-09 01:28:36 could have gone to detriot
2006-05-09 01:29:40 why you make delphi kettering your base

4.1 A photograph of the final two pages of Thomas Claburn's/ AOL user 23187425's *i feel better after i type to you* (2006). No changes have been made to the text.

As a curation of these sombre and plodding search entries, *i feel better after i type to you* remediates the leaked personal data into *information.* Here, "data" refers to unorganized individual units of raw material that do not carry any specific meaning, whereas "information" refers to a group of data that are organized within a context so as to collectively become usable for human purposes. Claburn's aesthetic effort thus turns the *data* of user 23187425 into *information.*

By curating the massive leak data into information, and into a poem, Claburn establishes an interesting type of intimacy between a human and information technology. The title and the premise of *i feel better after i type to you* takes the vulnerability of user 23187425's public exposure, and makes it personal for the reader of the book. This intimacy involves relational dynamics like setting boundaries around privacy and sharing. The larger issue at hand, however, is that our information technologies are inherently "promiscuous," even in the absence of privacy gaffes like AOL's data leak. Their boundaries are porous. They systematically and routinely "leak" our data, and must do so in order to effectively communicate, to make meaning, with us and each other: "Every wireless network card downloads/reads in all packets it can and then erases those not directly addressed to it; if it is running in 'promiscuous' mode, it also writes these packets forward to its central processing unit ... This promiscuity means that every user has probably downloaded all sorts of illegal materials. Your network card is, technically speaking, initially 'slutty': dirty, open to all traffic, indiscriminate (to clean is to delete). Crucially, though, without this necessary vulnerability/openness, there would be no Internet, no communications" (Chun and Friedland 2015, 4–5). In order to make data meaningful, for it to become information, it must be carefully corralled and curated into a system. But in order to perform an act of communication, the data must be promiscuous and leaky; it must escape our attempts at curation. What this means is that our general degree of indifference to our own data vulnerabilities is not only pragmatic, but functional. Allowing our data to leak, to escape the bounds of our care, to be exposed in the info-sphere, allows our data to be seen by others. We expose ourselves to be observed, or witnessed, by corporate entities and peers alike. It was this kind of "participatory" (Albrechtslund 2008) surveillance that went into the making of *i feel better after i type to you.* Once exposed, our data then have the possibility of being taken up by other users in other systems of organization, becoming information with meaning.

As an aesthetic response to an overload of information, *i feel better after i type to you* expands the discussion that sees the mutual exposure of human and machine actors to each other as an affecognitive amplifier of overload boredom and habitual practice; I wish to factor in our tolerance for information promiscuity and vulnerability for the sake of not just being "connected," but being *witnessed* ("watched over by machines of loving grace" [Brautigan 1967]). We can use *i feel better after i type to you* like a prism that refracts questions about the risks we tolerate in order to get intimate with machines, make meaning out of information overload, and so process our boredom. The poem makes perceptible the ways in which overload boredom is not merely a by-product of an info-tech age – a disjunction between the speed of technology and our own slow bodies – but rather, is a disaffective medium of the collective in which we try to manifest parts of ourselves to be accessed by others. Doing so, however, requires a reframing of information theory and its relationship to boredom so we can explicate the means by which this manifestation happens, and show why it is worthy of being understood.

* * *

OVERLOAD BOREDOM AND SHARED ENTROPY

2006-05-09 02:14:43 out of all mine
2006-05-09 02:15:41 go to bed
2006-05-09 02:16:16 if i work hard i don't think off
2006-05-09 02:17:29 left my computer down
2006-05-09 02:17:59 work hard
2006-05-09 02:19:11 get some sleep
2006-05-09 02:19:44 work tommorr
...
2006-05-09 02:31:11 not a poor woman
2006-05-09 02:31:52 i have to work
2006-05-09 02:32:19 i have to work
2006-05-09 02:32:56 no dates no fun
2006-05-09 02:34:10 ready for bed
2006-05-09 02:34:37 not across
2006-05-09 02:35:09 not a cross
(AOL user 23187425 and Claburn 2006, 28–9)

We might imagine online meandering at 2 AM as both a cause and symptom of boredom. But overload boredom as a problem of the relationship between meaning and information points to questions beyond the subjectivity of user 23187425. For instance, how can we describe what is going on in the dumping of all manner of intensely personal data into the vulnerable repository of a search bar and the systems networked with it? To find out, we must pause and ask: what *is* information?

Information, Meaning, and Boredom

In the pre-Internet age, sociologist Orrin Klapp made a direct link between boredom and information overload, writing: "meaning and interest [information] are found mostly in the mid-range between extremes of … banality [boredom] and noise [entropy]" (1986, 2). With "any gain in banality or noise" there comes "meaning loss and boredom" (2). This is Klapp's way of accounting for a critical loss of meaning in modern society, conceived in terms of a "lag" where the slow process of meaning-making cannot catch up with rapid accretion of information – information overload.[4]

For Klapp, information is not inherently meaningful. Rather, he conceives of information as a consequence of actions that perform a "reduction of uncertainty [entropy] in any binary (yes-or-no) choice, commonly measured in bits" (Klapp 1982, 58). Information is about getting a clearer understanding of the choices available to us. Information *becomes meaningful* only when it enters and relates "to a pattern or scheme of which one is part," and this relating to a pattern or scheme is "an awareness that is necessarily subjective" (Klapp 1982, 58). Thus, information is a "fast horse,"[5] while meaning is a slow and careful one that lags behind. Meaning grows via a holistic process – a deeply synthetic process – while information merely accumulates. It is additive, which is why it can overload us. The crisis of meaning is the consequence of information hitting us so fast and so hard that it loses its organizational structure – it disintegrates into a form of "data" in need of contextualizing.

Framing the meaning crisis as a problem of speed, processing, and information production, allows us to see that human bandwidth for processing information might vary with technology, individuals, and groups, but our need for organizing and curating this information is a bottleneck that limits our ability to sort stimuli, and so, to make meaning.[6] Therefore, it is inevitable that meaning-making will be "slow or insufficient compared with the speed and amount of information accumulating in modern society" (Klapp 1982, 61–2). And if meaning is identified with holistic synthesis of information, and boredom is identified with its loss through entropy, then we had better clarify the range of meanings of the concept "information," and their relationships to entropy. We need a comprehensive theory of information to get a better grasp on how an overload of information makes information less meaningful – mystifying, even.

Information versus Entropy

In writing about information theory, the terms "information" and "entropy" are commonly used interchangeably, or even to modify each other, as in the phrase "*informational entropy*" (Collins 2002, emphasis mine). But if "information" is meant to be that which clears away whatever obfuscates meaning by *reducing entropy*, then how can the term "information" substitute or modify the term "entropy"? Understanding how this is possible requires that we change the angle from which we view entropy (uncertainty). For this, I will draw on Christoph Adami (2016), who provides a conversational and intuitive take on information that we can adopt for our purposes.

Adami describes information as "what allows you (who is in possession of that information) to make predictions with accuracy better than chance" (2016, 1–2). To *have* information "means that you know something. About something" (4). But that knowledge is not *necessarily* meaningful. That is because making meaning requires you not just to "know a thing" but know a thing in relation to the vast amount of stuff you do not know, in other words, to know that information's relationship to entropy. Whereas information is what "allows us to make predictions about a system we don't know … based on what states the system can take on," entropy quantifies how much is *not known* about that system (Adami 2016, 2). Entropy – the unknown, our uncertainty about a system – depends on the state of the observer. It depends on what you choose to measure,[7] what is perfectly measurable, what measurement instruments you use, and how many states they can resolve. Through measurement, you gain information. That means that entropy is *potential information*. Exactly how much information you gain in measurement is the difference between your uncertainty before you measured, minus the uncertainty after you

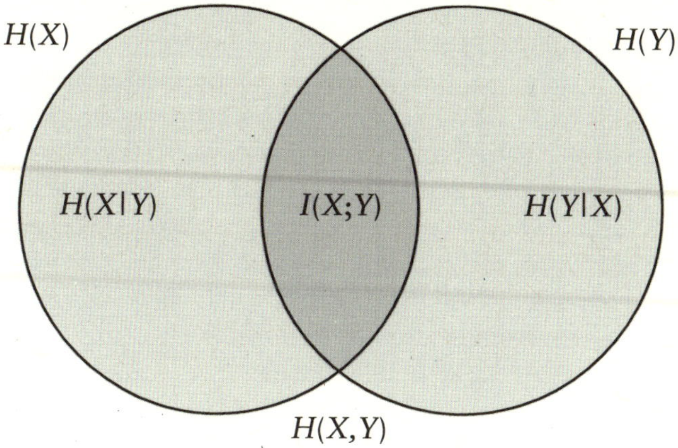

4.2 Entropy Venn diagram shows conditional and mutual entropies of two variables.

measured. But "in order to quantify how much you do not know, you have to know something about the thing you do not know" (Adami 2016, 10). How can we know something about the thing we do not know? We have to rely on conditional probabilities. Every assay toward information is dealing with conditional probabilities for the states of a system. Therefore, information itself is unconditional entropy minus conditional entropy.[8]

In the Venn diagram for two variables X and Y, the left circle represents the entropy of X (what is unknown about X), while the right circle represents the entropy of Y (what is unknown about Y). The area of overlap in the centre is "the shared entropy I (X : Y), which is what X knows about Y. Also what Y knows about X" (Adami 2016, 11). This means that another way of defining information is "shared entropy,"[9] an inter-agential check. The problem is when the shared entropy expands beyond our ability to recognize it as such. When the entropy becomes so great, the information becomes mere data, increasing uncertainty and disconnection. Our act of "sharing" becomes a driver of our overload boredom.

PRESENCING OUR SHARED ENTROPY

As a concept, shared entropy begins to help clarify the relationship between information overload and overload boredom. In the previous chapter I described how texting reproduces the disaffective conditions of overload boredom by keeping the variables of choice and information unpredictable and always in play. Sharing our information online, what I call "presencing," does the same, though it does so differently according to the various affordances of social media services, surveillance assemblages, and other information technologies.[10] The rampant information production that occurs by these means is, in other words, an amplification of shared entropy. So while boredom, in Klapp's formulation, increases as entropy increases, *overload boredom increases as shared entropy increases.* Ironically, as we will see through my reading of *i feel better after i type to you*, online presencing ends up as a paradoxical attempt to solve the meaning crisis – the spiritual crisis – of overload boredom with the information production (presencing, increasing shared entropy) that caused it in the first place.

So what is happening when user 23187425 is typing into the ether? We could say that user 23187425 is giving over data to a system, establishing shared entropy, presencing. In this sense, data corresponds with entropy, as it is potential information, and when we *share entropy*, we get information. If we think of information as "former uncertainty" minus "current uncertainty," then making our presence known through the information we share, making ourselves surveillable, is to *share* our uncertainty. Giving our personal data, merging it with larger sets from which statistical patterns emerge, places us in the centre of Adami's Venn diagram.[11] So we could say user 23187425 is risking what this leaky, surveillant system might do with their personal matters for the sake of cooperating with technology to cast their lot in with others – humans, machines, and avatars of ourselves – thereby turning their entropy into *shared* entropy. Yet, putting a presence online – by querying search engines, or sharing through social media – contributes to the increase of both shared entropy (information) and entropy proper (uncertainty). This is because as we increase the contents of systems that are already defined, we are also augmenting the info-sphere – gassing its atmosphere, raising the PSI of overload boredom.

To cast overload boredom in terms of shared entropy may conjure the warm-and-fuzzy emotional register denoted by the so-called "sharing economy," but this sharing is haunted by the spectre of disaffective withdrawal mentioned in chapter 2. We must take a frank look at the intransigent human impulse to form a system of references (networking apps, streaming platforms, discussion forums, etc.) to which one belongs, even if that belonging is dangerous and ill-considered. If boredom is a problem of meaning in relating self to world, then we could read online presencing as an orienting strategy of creating reference points in the world that refer back to the self, thus embedding the self in a context where meaning can be made. But multiplying the self in this way both orients and disorients; it amplifies the disaffect of overload boredom even as it seeks to address the problem of social fragmentation that is part of its spiritual crisis.

* * *

As the case of user 23187425 demonstrates, to give over information to a system is to create objects which, while related to the self, go on to have their own uncanny lives, lives through which we can also then live vicariously. For instance, by putting up a social web presence, or at least failing to prevent one from being rendered in our likeness from our digital footprint, our selves are subjected to surveilling scrutiny of social, corporate, and state agencies. The social relations through which we are constituted get obfuscated, seeming to derealize into forces invisible and unverifiable – and we might sense that we are losing reality proportionally. As Henry Giroux (2014) observes, "in the age of the self-absorbed self and its mirror image – selfie – intimacy becomes its opposite" – intimacy becomes withdrawal. "The exit from privacy becomes symptomatic of a society that gives up on [a] social and historical memory" of the goods privacy affords us, namely, the possibility of intimacy with *ourselves* (Giroux 2014).[12] We give this up in exchange for the possibility that withdrawal from the realm of the private reduces uncertainty about ourselves. Thus, surveillance both is *done to us* and also we *do ourselves* through it; withdrawal from privacy trades interiority for witness. It is a dubious trade, but a reasonable desire. It is an attempt to curate oneself in the context of others – maybe not consciously, maybe not always for specific people to see, but partly in order to feel like society has not moved on without us, without our contribution.

Reading *i feel better after i type to you* with information, entropy, and presencing in mind gives us reasons for what user 23187425 and what Claburn were doing, but reasons are not the whole causal picture. As the artist Robert Morris put it, "we will never find reasons both sufficient and necessary for actions" (1993, 618). But the aesthetic-affective speculation we are engaging here suggests another kind of analysis. The rhythm of our interactions with search engines is normally one of call and response – the searcher sends out a phrase and a cacophony of search results reply in their different voices. In *i feel better after i type to you*, the syncopation of the machine voice drops out. As stereo becomes mono, we are left with a "soliloquy" or monologue "of more than 8,200 queries" (Claburn in Dworkin and Goldsmith 2011, 138). Many of these are questions apparently addressed to someone called "joe" or "joseph." There are also multiple variations of certain statements and descriptive phrases typed out back to back or else in short succession; perhaps this was user 23187425 trying to get their words right for this "real" or "imagined" joe, but it could also be read as though user 23187425 was trying to optimize their wording for the search engine's logic.[13] While the conscious mind of user 23187425 would likely know that joe would never receive these digital missives, their fingers nonetheless tapped it all out, moving out of the body a loop of frustrated affects.

Timestamps attest to the way this torrent of typing came rapidly, half-formed, as if unbidden. Time in *i feel better after i type to you* is represented as passing according to the time of self-production. Time gets recalibrated as a collaboration between machine cognition, other-than-conscious processing, and the conscious action of typing. Insofar as the external information environment is not well matched to the internal metronome of our affecognitive circuits, we have to constantly adjust. User 23187425's search log can be seen as an implicit measure of the discrepancy between their intention and the result, and the unarticulated steps between thoughts. The user literally types about disconnection, longing for companionship, getting through the repetition of workday cycles, and being fed up by the meaningless choices (e.g., between work outfits) they offer. The log ticks forward according to the intervals of human thought which are the times from the formation of one thought to the next, and according to the speed of typing, and the speed of search result retrieval, and all the work of thinking that is mostly not conscious and cannot be.[14]

These rapid-shot fragments engender "a textual proximity" that, like affects, are "constructed below the level of the word to situate the language material within the potential turbulence of word parts, thereby allowing them to resonate both as entities and events" (McCaffery 2012, 159). As a literary object, the poem clarifies what is usually occluded in the gap between conscious and other-than-conscious processing. The human-machine collaboration in *i feel better after i type to you* devises a language that offers itself to other-than-intentional experience; the words become sensuous and relational.

In what might otherwise be a boring collection of random searches from a random user online, we begin to recognize in this human-machine interaction the intensification of an intransigent[15] capacity for bearing and seeking witness, and the necessity of and habituating to surveillance as a part of this search.

While user 23187425 would likely know that neither joe nor the AOL search engine would reciprocate their appreciation for feeling better after typing, the result is still a collaboration. It is a kind of conversation, though a conversation where the other party has become reticent; but maybe the algorithm was listening just as it was expected to. If we imagine this conversation between user 23187425 and the AOL search engine, we can imagine user 23187425 conversing with the search engine in order to cope with the disaffects of melancholy, loneliness, exhaustion, and a surfeit of sameness in the choices of daily life. On the other side, we can imagine the data breach as the search engine responding in its own way; first, by curating all of user 23187425's typing into timestamped semantic packets, but later, by violating the seal of confession in the data breach.

Claburn, on the other hand, as co-author, manifests other affective dynamics through his "uncreative" poetics. The poem shows why, as a user of texting apps or search engines or social media, we might feel better after we type to each other, but also that the affects of this activity are shaped by habituating to the uncertainty of information overload, the withdrawal from privacy, and the building pressure of overload boredom. *i feel better after i type to you* evokes user 23187425's habitual withdrawing from their own interiority alongside their uncertain connection to the info-sphere that envelops us. In the end, user 23187425 did not use the search engine for retrieving information as we normally conceive it. Instead, the search engine was a vehicle to share entropy – a way to use information that might relieve the disaffect of overload boredom for user 23187425, even though, ironically, it would amplify its pressure.

5

Information Enchantment

The Mystifying and the Kēdic

> I can't think anyone really believes that today's so-called 'information society' is just about information. Everyone knows it's about something else, way down … Living people do not speak much of the dull. Of those parts of life that are and must be dull. Why this silence? Maybe it's because the subject is, in and of itself, dull … only then we're again right back where we started, which is tedious and irksome. There may, though, I opine, be more to it … as in vastly more, right here before us all, hidden by virtue of its size.
>
> David Foster Wallace, *The Pale King*

The Pale King (2011) is a book about boredom:[1]

> "Irrelevant" Chris Fogle turns a page. Howard Cardwell turns a page. Ken Wax turns a page. Matt Redgate turns a page. "Groovy" Bruce Channing attaches a form to a file. Ann Williams turns a page. Anand Singh turns two pages at once by mistake and turns one back which makes a slightly different sound. David Cusk turns a page. Sandra Pounder turns a page. Robert Atkins turns two separate pages of two separate files at the same time. Ken Wax turns a page. Lane Dean Jr turns a page … A yawn proceeds across one Chalk's row by unconscious influence. Ryne Hobratschk turns a page. Latrice Theakston turns a page. Rotes Group Room 2 hushed and brightly lit, half a football field in length … Boris Kratz bobs with a slight Hassidic motion as he crosschecks a page with a column of figures. Ken Wax turns a page. Harriet Candelaria turns a page. Matt Redgate turns a page. Ambient room temperature 80° F … Joe "The Bastard" Biron-Maint turns a page. Ed Shackleford

> opens a drawer and takes a moment to select just the right paperclip ... Olive Borden turns a page. Rosellen Brown turns a page. Ken Wax turns a page. Devils are actually angels. (Wallace 2011, 310–14)

According to the purported narrator of the book – a mischievous character named David Wallace – the novel is "about negotiating boredom as one would a terrain, its levels and forests and endless wastes" filled with "dullness, information, and irrelevant complexity" (Wallace 2011, 85).[2] David Foster Wallace's posthumous tome indexes the culture of institutions dedicated to collecting huge stocks of information and how their bureaucratic logics bleed into culture at large. The book spends over five hundred pages, including footnotes and footnotes to footnotes, on the bureaucratic minutiae of the IRS. Much of Wallace's site-specific detail in the tax offices of Peoria, Illinois, is offered not because it is particularly compelling or provocative but because it is *not* inherently interesting. Instead, it is a voluntary encounter with boredom so that it can become a threshold for a reencounter with meaning, a kind of contemplative engagement with the anodyne features of our everyday lives that normally whiz by unnoticed.

Despite its setting in the pre-Internet mid-eighties mid-West, *The Pale King* is very much of its own post-Y2K moment, so it is not hard to see the fears and obsessions of contemporary hyperlinked data culture in the experience of its characters and construction of its world.[3] Main characters like the so-called "fact psychic" Claude Sylvanshine behaves like a search engine gone haywire, automatically and randomly "downloading" discrete facts into his memory banks. Or there is the character nicknamed "Irrelevant" Chris Fogle, who can call up an exhaustive account of just about any IRS policy with the same ease as detailing a moment of his own personal biography. The effect of Wallace's characters rattling off IRS policy is unusually anonymizing for characters in a novel, with whom a reader is used to identifying, or villainizing, or at least getting to know as a person, rather than as a cog in a machine, or line of code in an algorithm.

It is apparent that the interior lives of Wallace's characters – their family lives, their social, and of course their work lives – are all colonized by professional practice and the rituals they have sanctified in order to endure it. The way they "express themselves" conforms entirely to the language and structures of "the service" (i.e., the IRS).[4]

Yet, the characters' bureaucratic attention to thoroughness and procedure ironically winds up being confessional.[5] The histories and psychologies of these characters become the metadata that describe where the information came from and how and why it was acquired. As each of these data points spin off in the circular manner of indexed reference materials, Wallace's terrain of boredom comes to brim with dullness, information, and irrelevant complexity. Through these byzantine stories, *The Pale King* exposes the everythingness of contemporary info-capitalist interconnections, and therefore, the arbitrariness of any singular moment or idea that we might orient ourselves towards as inherently meaningful.

AESTHETICIZING (OVERLOAD) BOREDOM

In form and content, *The Pale King* exposes the meaninglessness of everything, and the overload boredom that develops as a result, with a view to finding meaning within that bleak exposure. As Wallace writes in the epigraph above, the living do not speak much of the dull. This problem arises from the human relationship to what I characterize in this chapter as the enchantments of information as mediated by overload boredom. In chapter 2 I argued that living people cyclically withdraw from the dullness of overload boredom so that it passes beneath mention, hidden by virtue of its size, while in chapters 3 and 4 I applied an aesthetic speculative inquiry to art objects that resist withdrawing from overload boredom and find ways instead to make meaning with its disaffects and surplus information.

The Pale King, like *W8ING* and *i feel better after i type to you*, uses the surplus of information – information overload – as material to work with, play with, and to comment on our experiences of boredom in bureaucratic environments. The fictional tax workers of the book speak endlessly about the dull, to the living reader, who under other circumstances would probably run from such a huge – near to absurd – volume of information about the IRS. Yet, Wallace fictionalizes and produces art with that information. In this way – in both form and content – Wallace runs close to the mode of antiexpressive writing, introduced in the previous chapter, in the way that conceptual poet Kenneth Goldsmith (2008a) describes as using tactics of "uncreativity, unoriginality, illegibility, appropriation, plagiarism, fraud, theft, and falsification as its precepts; information management, word processing, databasing, and extreme process as its methodologies – and boredom as its ethos." While *The Pale King*'s form as a novel limits its use of some of these antiexpressive tactics, it nevertheless submits to algorithmic rules and enabling constraints in order to embrace boredom.[6]

For example, while Wallace demonstrates a constraint-based methodology by giving his characters pages and pages of stream-of-consciousness monologuing, he did not compose any of the novel using a process like "automatic writing."[7] And while Wallace does not "cite" actual IRS forms in the mode of "found writing," he does make use of an IRS aesthetic by crafting an entire chapter of *The Pale King* in two columns to look like a policy document. He could have recreated or re-presented a great deal of IRS ephemera, but he did not use actual boilerplate. By taking classes in accounting Wallace filled his pages with the tortuous bureaucratic language and logics of IRS policy, instead of copying and pasting existing forms.

Similarities in Form; Differences in Value

The Pale King might share certain formal features of antiexpressivist writings, but its aesthetic *values* differ in meaningful ways, most importantly, with respect to boredom.[8] *The Pale King* encourages the reader to get *care*ful and contemplative with boredom, perceive it, feel it, know it. To show exactly how *The Pale King* does so, it is worth continuing to make a contrast with the way antiexpressivist values shape artists' and audiences' encounters with information and boredom in their work. To wit, the antiexpressivists try to unbore boredom, to find unexpected joy in repetition and blandness, rather than coming to terms with the disaffective qualities of overload.

For example, many antiexpressivist writings reject the need for their semantic content to be consumed in order to communicate or indeed to achieve their full realization as art objects.[9] Instead, all such writings ask of the audience is to understand their *premise*. This is because with conceptual art "all of the planning and decisions are made beforehand and the execution is a perfunctory affair" (LeWitt 1967, 79).[10] What these artists value is that the audience gets the idea,[11] because the value of the work is to challenge "the nature of the art object, the qualifications for being an artist, the fundamental role of art in its various institutional contexts, and the proper scope of activities for the audience" (Dworkin 2011, xxv). Therefore, understanding the premise, knowing the algorithm the artist is following, is enough for the piece to matter – a conceptual work like John Baldessari's *I Will*

Not Make Any More Boring Art is a work about boredom where you can conceptually relate to boredom, but do not have to feel bored. With works like these, you do not necessarily have to read every line or word and actually experience the tedium of that reading, though if you imagine the work it took to create the art – if you imagine its making – then you gain something (see figure 5.1).

Within antiexpressive writing, in particular, the focus on *premise* rather than consumption or intimate encounter results in the boredom of its "ethos" being a somewhat distanced and intellectually abstract version of boredom. Antiexpressive methodologies of "information management, word processing, databasing, and extreme process" mean that its encounters with boredom may expose the sociotechnical causes of the "boredom that haunts the Western world" (Goodstein 2005, 1), without engaging the affective consequences of that haunting, and its demonic strangeness. While they may help us think about the circumstances of this information's production, as Claburn's piece did in the preceding chapter,[12] they allow withdrawal to remain the key experiential texture in relating to boredom arising from information overload.

In stark contrast, *The Pale King*'s algorithm does not condone withdrawal – it requires its user (reader) to *participate* by having affecognitive experiences with the semantic content of the novel, which, as a genre, expects that you read it front to back, completely. Using narrative to stabilize the reader's attention to tedious information, Wallace short circuits our habitual withdrawal from overload boredom. Whereas conceptual art is a matter of setting up a system and stepping back as it runs its course (Dworkin 2011, xliv), Wallace does not restrict the aesthetic values of his work to an algorithmic *premise*. As his David Wallace narrator character says: "I am about art here, not simple reproduction" (Wallace 2011, 259).

The semantic content of *The Pale King* – its characters and stories – involves the author, reader, and book in a relation of care. Wallace cares about his work. He cares about his readers' engagement with his work. He cares about the cultural consequences of that engagement:

> Sarcasm, parody, absurdism and irony are great ways to strip off stuff's mask and show the unpleasant reality behind it. The problem is that once the rules of art are debunked, and once the unpleasant realities the irony diagnoses are revealed and diagnosed, "then" what do we do? Irony's useful for debunking

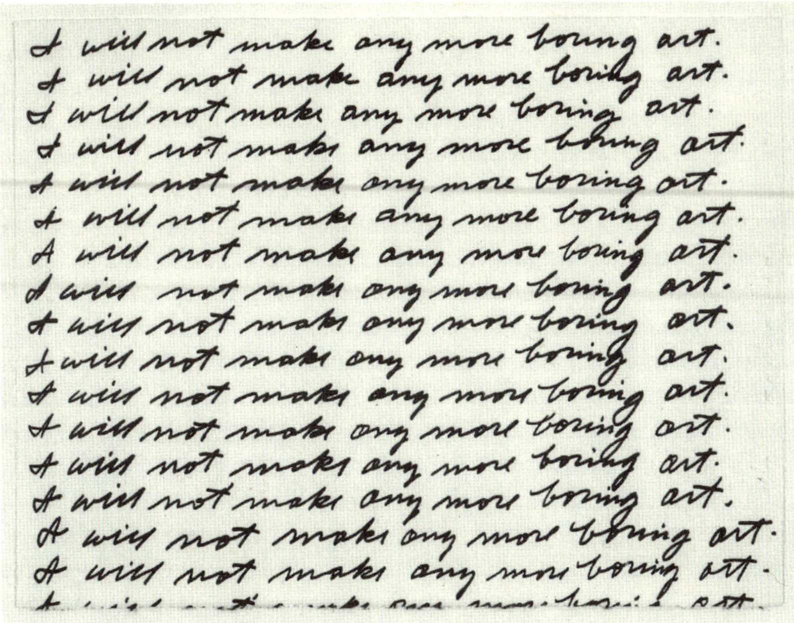

5.1 John Baldessari's lithograph *I Will Not Make Any More Boring Art* (1971, 57 x 76.4 cm) is based on an installation created at Nova Scotia College of Art and Design (NSCAD). The original installation was carried out by students Baldessari had instructed to write the phrase on the white gallery walls, like punishment on a school blackboard, in his stead, since there was no money to fly him out to Nova Scotia.

> illusions, but most of the illusion-debunking in the U.S. has now been done and redone. Once everybody knows that equality of opportunity is bunk and Mike Brady's bunk and Just Say No is bunk, now what do we do? All we seem to want to do is keep ridiculing the stuff. Postmodern irony and cynicism's become an end in itself, a measure of hip sophistication and literary savvy. Few artists dare to try to talk about ways of working toward redeeming what's wrong, because they'll look sentimental and naive to all the weary ironists. Irony's gone from liberating to enslaving. There's some great essay somewhere that has a line about irony being the song of the prisoner who's come to love his cage. (Wallace 1993)

Wallace dares to "redeem" our relationships to the "stuff" in our media ecology.[13] Moreover, he is critical of those artists and critics who made an end of irony, cynicism, sarcasm, parody, and absurdism, in part because of the way they used boredom as an affective medium to distance themselves from discomfiting ambivalence. As the art historian Julian Jason Haladyn puts it, such work leverages "the meaninglessness of boredom as a mediating factor in the relationship between the subjective and the objective realities within modern culture" (2008, 6). This conceptually distanced mode of boredom then becomes the boredom of audiences, too. According to Wallace: "the well-conditioned viewer [does not want to leave themselves] open to others' ridicule by betraying passé expressions of value, emotion, or vulnerability ... The well-trained lonely viewer becomes even more allergic to people. Lonelier ... Genuine human encounters seem even scarier ... [One learns to wear a] blank, bored, too-wise expression ... for tomorrow's excruciating ride on the brightly lit subway, where crowds of blank, bored-looking people have little to look at but each other" (Wallace 1997, 63). We can read Wallace's critique of boredom *as a disaffective withdrawal from the info-sphere's surplus of semiotic products and the tyranny of choosing among them* (i.e., information overload). In other words, it is not boredom per se that Wallace is criticizing here, but a certain way of relating to it.

In *The Pale King*, Wallace shows the double nature of boredom – in the same way that thinkers like Heidegger, Benjamin, and Lefebvre did before him – where, in one mode, in the indifference of boredom, nothing matters, and in another, boredom gives insight into the endless creative possibility of our existence. What this means is that *The Pale King* guides the reader in a slow movement *through* the latter mode of boredom. The book offers a prolonged opportunity to reflect on the insight of one of its characters, Chris Fogle, about how humans should respond to information overload: since "the world and reality [i]s already essentially penetrated and formed," its "constituent info generated ... now a meaningful choice lay in herding, corralling, and organizing that torrential flow of info" (Wallace 2011, 240). This curatorial impulse is how *The Pale King* produces, instead of merely speaks of, the psychic pain of boredom.

While *The Pale King* allows very little to happen in the active present in order for the book to be painfully dull for large tracts, it also glitters here and there with the sheer precision of capturing how experiences of boredom *feel*; what it is like to commute on an airless bus, to sit in a windowless room, to process a bottomless stack of tasks. The glittering beauty allows us to get affecognitively intimate with boredom, instead of withdraw from it.[14]

The only way out of *The Pale King*'s boredom, which is caused by an overload of information, is through a sincere engagement with it. An engagement that helps define a system that organizes the torrential flows of *information overload* in order to turn its irrelevant complexity into *information* – to reduce entropy, allowing for meaning-making. This is Wallace's curatorial ethos. Using enabling constraints like its info-culture tropes and techniques like citationality, *The Pale King* invokes the characters' sense of overload, and offers it to the reader. We see this technique in the way characters in the novel materialize overload boredom, capturing moments of its sensory qualities before overload can distract us from observing it directly, leaving us with its afterimage. So, rather than merely valuing its premise of being a book "about boredom," *The Pale King* carefully exercises the readers' capacity for boredom, attending to the *feeling and perceiving* of boredom, in what I call an "aestheticizing askēsis."[15]

AESTHETICIZING ASKĒSIS: A RESPONSE TO OVERLOAD BOREDOM

In his dealing with boredom, Wallace's sincerity and earnestness put him in line with the monks of antiquity who were willing to wrestle with the Noontide Demon of boredom using spiritual exercises known as askēsis. The concept of askēsis (origin of the modern English "ascetic") refers to a "regular daily programme" for the monks "that ma[de] possible a gradual transformation of the self" (Gale 2017). These exercises involved self-research, investigation, telling the complete truth about oneself, attentiveness (meaning presence to others and presence to oneself), and reading (ibid.). This rigorous practice both responded to and gave rise to a unique affective quality they called akēdia. "Akēdia is a privative formed on the abstract noun kēdia which is itself derived from the more concrete kēdos, one of an expansive lexicon of Greek words for care and concern" (Gale 2017). Akēdia signified feeling bored with the cultivation of subjectivity and with the spiritual exercises used to respond to that feeling. The modern notion of boredom traces back to this affecognitive discomfort associated with slow and careful cultivation of subjectivity. *The Pale King* refers obliquely to these spiritual exercises in its vignettes of workplace boredom, but much more importantly, it puts the reader through them.

The reader's encounter with the length and bureaucratic density of *The Pale King* echoes the way that the Noontide Demon, the pre-modern embodiment of boredom himself, was known to trouble "the ascetic's ability to sustain reading and the central place reading had within askēsis" (Gale 2017).[16] We see this in the example offered by the ascetic Evagrius, who described the struggle of a monk against the Noontide Demon: "When he reads, the one afflicted with acedia yawns a lot and readily drifts off into sleep; he rubs his eyes and stretches his arms; turning his eyes away from the book, he stares at the wall and again goes back to reading for a while; leafing through the pages, he looks curiously for the end of texts, he counts the folios and calculates the number of gatherings. Later, he closes the book and puts it under his head and falls asleep, but not a very deep sleep, for hunger then rouses his soul and has him show concern for its needs" (in Gale 2017). Wallace riffs on this soporific moment when he has his lapsed Christian character Lane Dean fall asleep on the job and receive a demonic visit from boredom.[17] While working silently processing tax returns among a room full of silent people processing tax returns, Dean begins contemplating his boredom, fights it, and loses. In this overworked vision, the entity – "the phantom," Dean calls it – appeared to be "a big older fellow with a seamed face and picket teeth" (382). But the phantom was oneirically indistinct and "kept moving his upper body around in a slight kind of shape or circle, and the movements left a little bit of a visual trail" (382). Speaking not quite *to* Dean, the phantom performs an etymology of the word boredom, explaining that in English there were "a good five hundred years of no word for it" (Wallace 2011, 383). The etymologically inclined apparition continued, saying: "No word for the Latin *accidia* made so much of by monks under Benedict. For the Greek ἀκηδία. Also, the hermits of third-century Egypt, the so-called *daemon meridianus*, when their prayers were stultified by pointlessness and tedium and a longing for violent death" (383).

Like Dean, and like the monks of akēdia, Wallace expects you to read. He expects you to be bored reading, and he expects you to work through that boredom. At 548 pages of tales about the tax world, *The Pale King* is an ascetic technology – a "spiritual exercise" of the sort that, under the right circumstances, could induce contemplative modes and altered states of consciousness.[18] *The Pale King* instigates boredom and then uses reading as a spiritual exercise to encourage the working through of your boredom. Askēsis, in this case, involves handling a heavy load of information and leads to the quasi-meditative trance entered by those devoted to faithful practice as reader and/or writer, consumer and/or producer. Wallace was most explicit about this process in a typed note that he left among his papers and the unfinished novel, which laid out the novel's idea: "Bliss – a-second-by-second joy and gratitude at the gift of being alive, conscious – lies on the other side of crushing, crushing boredom. Pay close attention to the most tedious thing you can find (Tax Returns, Televised Golf) and, in waves, a boredom like you've never known will wash over you and just about kill you. Ride these out, and it's like stepping from black and white into color. Like water after days in the desert. Instant bliss in every atom" (Wallace 2011, 548). But to achieve this "bliss in every atom" requires one to go through the slow, painful, encounter with akēdia caused by the overload of information in works like *The Pale King*. This is a process not without danger. We must be keenly aware of what makes the difference between a blissful experience, and a crippling, nearly fatal one.[19]

To understand this difference, we can again contrast Wallace and the abovementioned conceptualist Kenneth Goldsmith. For Goldsmith, the aesthetic solution to boredom might only work for artists, not for audiences. Goldsmith describes his experience of writing *Day*, a 900-page retyping one day's issue of the *New York Times*: "Far from being boring, it was the most fascinating writing process I've ever experienced. It was surprisingly sensual. I was trained as a sculptor and moving the text from one place to another became as physical, and as sexy as, say, carving stone. It became this wild sort of obsession to peel the text off the page of the newspaper and force it into the fluid medium of the digital" (Goldsmith 2004). As artist, Goldsmith "rides out the waves" by wrestling with boredom in the making of his work, but the work does not ask readers to wrestle in the same way. This is consistent with conceptual art's primary function being to challenge "fundamental assumptions of the art world" (Dworkin 2011, xxv). In other words, we could say that someone like Goldsmith attempts to achieve bliss by unboring boredom – which is tantamount to withdrawing from it. To avoid the pain of boredom, Goldsmith aestheticizes *akēdia,* he transmutes boredom into *interest*.

Wallace, on the other hand, does not give his audience space to withdraw from boredom by merely appreciating the premise of his work, because he knows that when you withdraw, you are only prolonging the inevitable encounter with "crushing, crushing boredom." Your future self is left to deal with the seriousness and totality of the information we encounter every day, regardless of whether we want to encounter it or not. Reading Wallace this way, reveals the futility of responding to the spiritual crisis of overload with avoidance and withdrawal. The "spiritual crisis" requires "spiritual exercise." But first you have to "see" the difference between the blissful – or kēdic – and the mystifying forms of overload, hence the need for *aestheticizing askēsis*. Wallace makes feeling bored spiritually significant; he makes the pain of boredom *meaningful*.

FROM ASKĒSIS TO ENCHANTMENT: KĒDIC AND MYSTIFYING ENCHANTMENT WITH INFORMATION OVERLOAD

As a consequence of *The Pale King*'s aestheticizing askēsis, it refracts information overload into two idioms of enchantment – the blissful, or what I call "kēdic" enchantment, and the disaffective, what I call "mystifying" enchantment. *The Pale King* shows how information overload enchants[20] in these two ways (kēdic, mystifying) using the strange – possibly supernatural – quirks belonging to its characters. These quirks embody and concretize the very personal effects exerted by very impersonal information systems: characters levitate, see demons, experience factual telepathy, and have machine-like memory. Their physiology acknowledges that information overload is profoundly strange, but ubiquitous; everywhere, but unfamiliar, foreign, bearing the fantastic potential of alternative realities. The characters' experiences of these quirks are poignant, but private. Their strangeness is unknown, except by the reader – perpetually obscured, disguised in the cracks of the information economy through which they keep falling. By keeping the characters' quirks private, Wallace does not disrupt the bureaucratic realism of the novel's world. (The narrator says: "All of this is true. This book is really true" [Wallace 2011, 69]). It is not a magical realist world. It is our world. This is what keeps the strangeness of the personal experience strange: the quirks make no sense in the otherwise workaday world of the story. The quirks are strange not by nature of their ontology, but by virtue of their context – as if the monks of akēdia had smartphones. But they make a lot of sense in our post-Internet age.

In the stories of characters like Claude Sylvanshine and Chris Fogle, Wallace shows narratively that the result of an encounter with information overload is either to be mystified by it or to get kēdic with it, and he encourages the kēdic. To this goal, he herds, corrals, and organizes a torrential flow of info generated by the attributes of these characters: Sylvanshine's "spontaneous data intrusions" and Fogle's "irrelevant" monologues. These strange attributes simultaneously generate the info, and function as the algorithms – the rules, enabling constraints – that determine whether the character experiences information overload as mystifying or kēdic.[21]

Kēdic Enchantment

When we have a set of enabling constraints to herd, corral, and organize a torrential flow of info, it is possible to treat those constraints as permission not to do anything other than the task at hand. We might be able to relax into this information immersion, as into a warm bath filling slowly. These constraints reduce a deluge to a thin stream of information. We might engage with this information in a careful and contemplative fashion. To surrender to the presence of a portion and let its mundane details absorb you is to create space for your imagination to intuit its connection to something larger and therefore patterned and interconnected, like stepping back from a pixelated image to see the characters form on a digital screen. This attunement is what I call "kēdic information enchantment." Kēdic enchantment attunes the disaffective medium of overload boredom towards the humane temporality of a premodern "relaxed, ancestral" boredom (re: Benjamin).

Mystifying Enchantment

In contrast, when we have an overload of information but no clear boundaries indicating what system it might be a part of, nor a standard of measurement (a filter for the information's usefulness), then that information becomes noise: we cannot use it to reduce our uncertainty about any system. When information dissolves into arbitrary patterns, it is not informative, it is instead mystifying. This mystification is not the ecstasy of the religious "mystic," but the obfuscation of political propaganda. It produces not insight, but entropy, where patterns of internal perception fail to cohere with the patterns that make up the external world. Instead of a thin stream, there is a firehose of information, and consequently, we withdraw from the blast. Without enabling constraints, simple volume and density disaffect the individual and their relationships to "stuff," the non-human-others encountered in the wilderness of the digital media ecology. What I call "mystifying information enchantment" attunes the disaffective medium of overload boredom towards its definitive feature of withdrawal.

Sylvanshine's Factual Telepathy: The Mystifying Enchantment of Overload

It is within the quirks of Claude Sylvanshine, the factual telepath, that we begin to see the effects of a mystifying enchantment with information overload. Sylvanshine functions like a search engine on the fritz, like a webpage full of pop-up ads, or a smartphone overheating from bulk data packets and signal transmissions. Since childhood, Sylvanshine has suffered "spontaneous data intrusions" whose "sudden flashes of insight or awareness are structurally similar to but usually far more tedious and quotidian than the dramatically relevant foreknowledge we normally conceive as ESP or precognition" (Wallace 2011, 118). The world Sylvanshine inhabits is already parsed into clear cut objects, about which there are unconstructed facts, self-evident and needing no interpretation in order to be expressed in language, as facts. Sylvanshine might learn "on, say, 12 July 1981, the precise metric weight and speed of a train moving southwest through Prešov, Czechoslovakia, at the precise moment he's supposed to be crosschecking 1099-INT receipts with the tax return of Edmund and Willa Kosice," about whom he unfortunately knows some dull factoids, as well (119). The content is overdetailed even as it is partial: "How long a piece of gum has resided on the underside of the third-row fourth-from-left seat of the Virginia Theater, Cranston RI, but not who put it there or why" (120–1). Sylvanshine knows "you don't chase these facts down; they're like lures that lead you nowhere. He's learned this from hard experience" (119). In the world of *The Pale King* one datum might be connected to the next in some arcane pattern, but it belongs to a system neither characters nor readers will ever be privy to.

The likening of Sylvanshine's data intrusions to psychic abilities like extra-sensory perception (ESP) and precognition is profoundly apropos in light of knowing what we know now about information: that information is that which allows the possessor to make predictions about a system with accuracy better than chance. It is accurate, then, to call Sylvanshine's intrusions "*data* intrusions" rather than "information intrusions." Not only are they not dramatically relevant in the way ESP or precognition are normally conceived to be, but they are not relevant at all to making predictions about systems with any greater-than-chance accuracy; it is impossible to know to which systems they pertain. In other words, each of these facts has a story, but they are coy about telling us what it is. Like hearing half of a telephone conversation, your brain starts trying to fill in the gaps, but cannot. It is agitating. Sylvanshine gets cognitions totally *estranged* from the experiences of his own life, and gets data that can do no work; he gets entropy, arbitrary patterns, ***mystifying information enchantment.***

More significantly, being privy to the context attached to the piece of gum on the underside of the theatre seat would be *just one more fact* that would not translate into predictive efficacy about anything the character (and therefore the reader) *cares about.* Even if the patterns became apparent, the data would "just sit there conveying nothing but their own shape" (Fish 2018). The facts are possible to verify, but the sheer volume of information is so great as to be prohibitive of verification. Whether at the scale of a state agency or an individual person, a system that has too much information cannot understand what it has.[22] It cannot turn the information into predictive value; into knowledge. And because no "care" is involved, because the information is not corralled within the kēdic bounds of askēsis, the result is a confrontation with the meaningless, the dull, the overwhelming: mystifying enchantment. Sylvanshine experiences this as: "an oceanic impression so literally obliterating that [he] was cast or propelled back in on himself and felt again the edge of the shadow of the wing of Total Terror and Disqualification pass over him, the knowledge of his being surely and direly ill-suited for whatever lay ahead, and of its being only a matter of time before this fact emerged and was made manifest to all those present in the moment that [he] finally, and forever, lost it" (Wallace 2011, 26). Sylvanshine exemplifies how the spiritual crisis of overload boredom consists in a mystifying enchantment with information overload. In other words, an estrangement – a disaffecting withdrawal – from the world of information which informs us, leaving us lonely, melancholic, and separated from all other beings, including ourselves. However, this crisis is only one side of the Möbius strip of overload boredom, as Wallace goes on to "redeem what's wrong" with our relationship to information by depicting what an askēsis might look like in a context of information overload.

The Kēdic Enchantment of "Irrelevant" Chris Fogle

At first glance, "Irrelevant" Chris Fogle appears, like Claude Sylvanshine, to be a fountain of data, not information. He recalls his own memories and the totality of IRS systems and procedures with equal facility. His uncanny "documentary" mode of encountering the world means he remembers everything in great detail, and lacks a filter that might separate his phenomenological perceptions from his bureaucratic archive. As a character he looks, "irrelevant" – "noisy." The David Wallace character diagnoses him as "logorrheic,"[23] saying he fails: "to understand is that there are vastly different kinds of truth, some of which are incompatible with one another. Example: A 100 percent accurate, comprehensive list of the exact size and shape of every blade of grass in my front lawn is 'true,' but it is not a truth that anyone will have any interest in. What renders a truth meaningful, worthwhile, & c. is its relevance, which in turn requires extraordinary discernment and sensitivity to context, questions of value, and overall point – otherwise we might as well all just be computers downloading raw data to one another" (Wallace 2011, 259). And for the majority of the novel, Fogle does appear to be irrelevant and noisy, contributing to the reader's own experience of overload. Until we hear that Fogle once had a major conversion – a road to Damascus moment[24] – that actually has given him discernment with respect to the relationship between data, information, and meaning with respect to his values.[25]

At one point, responding to some non-diegetic question that is evidently about how he got into "the Service," Fogle rambles for ninety-eight pages of exasperating detail. For the better part of the chapter, he describes drifting "for several years, in and out of three different colleges, one of them two different times, and four or five different majors. One of these might have been a minor. I was pretty much of a wastoid" (Wallace 2011, 154). His orbit of the adult world of work is thrown into various deformations by his distant relationship with his disappointed father and the conflict between his own nihilism and the suspicion that he is the only one in his postmodern world that is still concerned with sincere existential questions like alienation and meaning. Eventually, by accident of mixing up one nondescript college campus building for another, he stumbles into the final session of an advanced accounting class. The lecturer invites his listeners to embrace the tedium of the work for which they are training, and thereby at least ease the pain and temper the urge to be witnessed suffering it. The setting for this unusually dramatic moment is a classroom where business hats and briefcases figure prominently. The behaviour of all the other students is professionally immaculate. Fogle recounts the wise words of the professor in summing up the course: "True heroism is minutes, hours, weeks, year upon year of the quiet, precise, judicious exercise of probity and care – with no one there to see or cheer. This is the world ... Learn it now, or later – the world has time. Routine, repetition, tedium, monotony, ephemeracy, inconsequence, abstraction, disorder, boredom" (Wallace 2011, 230–1). It turns out that the professor was a Jesuit priest substituting for the regular instructor, which might explain the sermonic quality of his summary lecture.

As Marshall Boswell points out, the language of the priest-professor and Fogle's conversion and are drawn from a treatise on religious experience by the American pragmatist William James (*The Varieties of Religious Experience* [1902] 1977). In *Varieties,* James theorizes religious experience as "the feelings, acts, and experiences of individual men in their solitude, so far as they apprehend themselves to stand in relation to whatever they consider the divine" (in Boswell 2012, 474). The divine is what James defines as any "such primal reality as the individual feels impelled to respond to solemnly and gravely, and neither by a curse nor a jest" (in Boswell 2012, 474, with a wink to *Infinite Jest*). For the priest-professor in *The Pale King,* "the divine" corresponds to the kind of "world" he describes, and "heroism" is a result of coming to stand in proper relation to it – much as it was for James. These appeals to sincerity and individual purpose are ways in which James thought religious experience could offer an energy to life that it would otherwise lack. Insofar as Fogle finds a kēdic enchantment with information overload instead of being mystified by it, he finds Jamesian divinity in the fundamental elements of his data-based bureaucratic world.[26]

In Fogle's long-winded testimony he credits the priest-professor's speech with being the occasion of his own personal conversion to the calling of accountancy, laden as it was with insight about the nature of boredom, information, work, authority, and meaning. Yet, despite retaining his documentary mode of speaking in exhaustive detail, we can see that Fogle's spiritual revelation has brought him to terms with information overload: he has adopted an *ascetic practice of relating to it.* Therefore, in the end, despite his relatively mundane quirk, it is Fogle who ends up being the strangest character here, in that he can vocalize and make public his experience of this conversion. He achieves a kind of freedom from overload boredom in that he can meaningfully engage with information, rather than withdrawing from it.[27] Thanks to the substitute priest-professor, Fogle substitutes kēdia for mystification, realizing that he had been: "too free, or that this kind of freedom wasn't actually real – I was free to choose 'whatever' because it didn't really matter. But that this, too, was because of something I chose – I had somehow chosen to have nothing matter. It all felt much less abstract than it sounds to try to explain it … The point was that, through making this choice, I didn't matter, either. I didn't stand for anything. If I wanted to matter – even just to myself – I would have to be less free, by deciding to choose in some kind of definite way. Even if it was nothing more than an act of will" (225–6). For Fogle, the day-in-day-out dedication to sorting through data itself is elevated to a sort of spiritual vocation. The spiritual significance of the sorting "had something to do with paying attention and the ability to choose what [you] paid attention to, and to be aware of that choice, the fact that it's a choice" (189). Here we start to see a commensurability between the moral of Fogle, the unreliable David Wallace narrator, the substitute priest-professor, and Wallace's own honest-to-goodness advice in his famous *This Is Water* commencement address (Kenyon College 2005) where he seems to channel the priest-professor, saying: "the only thing that is 'capital T true' is that you get to decide what has meaning, what to worship."

A cynical reading would say: this is more obligatory self-making, more choice overload. But Fogle's conversion, the priest-professor's exhortation, and Wallace's advice are all rooted in the context of a/kēdia, and the root noun kēdos refers both to care for self and care for others. An ecological caring. Built into kēdia and akēdia is right relation between psychic interiority and affective collectivity.

Fogle's story is a kind of translation of kēdic practices from monastic antiquity into an information-age context where "self-care" is normally expressed in "secular" psychotherapeutic terms. The therapeutic milieu is not really divorced from Christian spirituality, however, since William James' pragmatic and experiential approach to self-development is a cornerstone of much "secular" self-help. In fact, the rise of modern psychology has gone hand-in-hand with unchurched spiritual traditions (Fuller 2001, 124). As Véronique Altglas puts it, "postpsychoanalytic therapies consider that solutions to life's problems lie in the change of individuals' attitudes, thereby making them responsible for their destiny … individuals' adaptation to their environment as the sine qua non for their self-realization" (2014, 206). Therapeutic culture tells us to turn inward, but to what?

Therapeutic culture cannot escape the forces and effects of info-capitalism. In fact, it caters to it. Info-capitalism channels our work of self-making towards using productivity therapeutics of stress-reduction, focus-enhancement, etc. We feed info-capitalism our information, and info-capitalism pays dividends. It gives us back an overload of information and choice. We withdraw from the overload and the withdrawal perpetuates the imperceptibility and lack of access to our interiority. However, thinking about the premodern context can help us understand our twenty-first century context differently, not, of course, that we can ever return to a premodern boredom. Nevertheless, the conceptual framework of a/kēdia can help us understand how to recognize the overloading effects of info-capitalism and use the resources overload boredom has within itself.

As in ancient akēdia, the fulcrum of boredom revolves around having to treat its resolution like a spiritual exercise. The only way out of boredom is through. In the twenty-first century, we first have to recognize overload boredom. It masks itself, but artists like Le Fraga, Claburn, and Wallace sometimes unmask it. We have to see that "the drives to novelty and innovation, speed and progress that have always defined modernity" still leave the Western world haunted by boredom (Goodstein 2005, 1) – no longer in its pre-modern or modern guise, but as overload boredom.

Imagine the Noontide Demon updated as the 24/7 Demon. Imagine these round-the-clock moments of texting, searching, and form-filling as encounters with this demon. Imagine relating to it so that these encounters get animated with a sense that our task is always greater than the one at hand. Our task is to resist the demon's mystification, and so to resist cycles of both self-making and self-effacing or self-anaesthetizing against – withdrawal from – the bombardments of overload. We have to see our choices about information as a matter of parsing out systems whose entropy we can reduce. We have to choose despite uncertainty and then come to terms with it afterwards; a kind of affecognitive curation. Our task is to not let the 24/7 Demon of overload boredom get away with cloaking itself while it mystifies us.

CODA: OF THOSE PARTS OF LIFE THAT ARE AND MUST BE DULL

> It's almost the opposite of awareness, if you think about it.
> I think this experience of accidental thinking is common, if
> perhaps not universal, although it's not something that you can
> ever really talk to anyone else about because it ends up being
> so abstract and hard to explain. Whereas in an intentional bout

> of concentrated major thinking, where you sit down with the conscious intention of confronting major questions like *"Am I currently happy?" or "What, ultimately, do I really care about and believe in?"* or – particularly if some kind of authority figure has just squeezed your shoes – "*Am I essentially a worthwhile, contributing type of person or a drifting, indifferent, nihilistic person?,*" then the questions often end up not answered but more like beaten to death, so attacked from every angle and each angle's different objections and complications that they end up even more abstract and ultimately meaningless than when you started. Nothing is achieved this way, at least that I've ever heard of. (Wallace 2011, 193)

There is an awareness in *The Pale King*, through a variety of characters, like Chris Fogle, to whom the above quote belongs, as well as the David Wallace narrator character, of the fact that Wallace's "be a good person" and "learn to pay attention" advice can land flat and awkward. In the words of literary critic Vadim Rizov, there can be "something unnervingly zealous about the way the novel addresses the perennial DFW concern of how to be a good person in a world full of aggravation, solipsism and distractions," and there is often a suspicion that the people who like Wallace's work are "undiscriminatingly or mindlessly worshipful" – a cynical perspective to which Risov disagrees.[28] Setting author persona and fandom aside, all I mean to claim here is that *The Pale King* has something to tell us about boredom that we rarely hear, from any quarter, and we can pull out of it something that is a lot more instructive than just "be a good person" and "learn to pay attention." The value is in the specific way that such a reading of *The Pale King* draws our attention to the information-overload context to which that advice pertains. It breaks the silence on those parts of life that are and must be dull.

To explore the possibilities of kēdic enchantment is not to advocate yet another personal, piecemeal solution such as those critiqued in chapter 2, insofar as it does not ignore the reality of our media ecology nor the need to ecologize the self. Chapter 2 showed the flawed conclusions that result when psychological treatments of boredom do not do the critical work of analyzing techno-social assemblages, like social media, for their power and affect in social institutions and the cultural forms to which they give rise. More importantly, though, these studies lack imagination about the technological systems themselves.

That is, psychological approaches to the problems of digital tech tend to rely on physiological causal explanations for those problems (e.g., the dopamine-addiction feedback loop activated by multitasking on your smartphone), and so they tend to yield behavioural action items that are not only personal, but eminently pragmatic. Yet overload is *enchanting*, and enchantment is, as Jane Bennett puts it, a complex and "*strange* combination of delight and disturbance" (2010, xi) "accompanied by a heightening of sensuous or aesthetic experience" (Bennett 2001, 37).

Of course we need mechanistic understandings of affecognition and behavioural levers for controlling it, but we also need conceptual paradigms that can help us affecognitively incorporate overload's strangeness. Cultivating an aesthetic-affective imagination about *systems* and our place in them, rather than meditating on the self as subject. Attuning to this kēdic enchantment, instead of coping with the mystifying enchantment, is a way of cultivating such imagination, making it an appropriately collective ethic for dealing with overload boredom.

6

Conclusion

Overload Boredom and a Hermeneutics of Care

The terrain of overload boredom can be cultivated. The information and irrelevant complexity that fill its levels, forests, and wastes can be curated. Some organizational system is needed to do so. My suggestion has been to, first, identify an array of affecognitive perceptions linked to information and choice overload: warped temporality; withdrawal from interiority; a suite of psychic pains: loneliness, melancholy, anxiety, and, of course, boredom. I collect these into a new concept: overload boredom. This concept enables us to identify its formal causes, such as key social institutions (info-capitalism), and their key values (self-making), and practices (habitual media use). It also allows us to take into account the material causes they are made of (namely, cellular and computational technology, and human affecognitive physiology). Noting these material causes has the felicitous effect of locating human agency among an ecology of nonhuman agencies – or better yet, it acknowledges agency is *distributed* among human and nonhuman beings.

The recognition of this distributed agency, the insight of seeing oneself as one among many agencies within our saturated media ecology allows us to perceive the ways we have withdrawn from the world and from ourselves. Remediating our relationships to this multiplicity of agents is the only way through the disaffect of overload boredom. We cannot just think our way out of overload, nor can we just feel our way out of it. Our task is aesthetic-affective speculation, in which we can draw on the resources of an aesthetic askēsis and the idiom of boredom as a "spiritual crisis" for a collective, and *care*ful form of thinking|feeling.

The askēsis imagined within *The Pale King* and practiced by the desert monks of antiquity involves a type of "self-care" not like the "self-*making*" encouraged by info-capitalism. Rather, what Wallace and the monks make visible is what we might call an ecological kind of self-*care* for the benefit of both the individual and the community. The monks were able to communicate this spiritual struggle because it existed conceptually within a shared cultural and theological framework. Yet today, even in a profoundly different media ecology, we are still contending with these problems of temporality and information. But unlike the monks who had nothing but time (and books) on their hands, for us there is too much stimulation and no sufficient shared framework for dealing with it. This is why a concept of *overload boredom as a spiritual crisis* is so important. It serves to curate and cultivate the information generated and consumed by the economic, social, and cultural arrangement of info-capitalism, which both asks too much and gives more than we can take. Thinking with the spiritual crisis of overload boredom is a way of collectively orienting toward meaningful choices regarding information overload, instead of withdrawing from the overload; making information out of entropy.

My goal all along has been to devise a way of organizing our information systems with our affecognitive physiology in mind – with the spiritual crisis of overload boredom in mind – so that we can do so with a "curator's" eye, rather than a(n info-)capitalist's eye. That is, an eye for meaning (discernment among semiotic artefacts with respect to context, value, and overall point), and not an eye for surplus (overload). Thus, against the hermeneutical nihilism of info-capitalism, and toward an ethics of care, I have modeled a kēdic hermeneutics.

READING THE BOOK FORWARD

Part of the arc of *The Spiritual Significance of Overload Boredom* is a movement that takes place through its art objects from the more concrete to the more abstract. I begin with social media at the deeply familiar scale of individual use (one-to-one texting); then move to a sort of meso scale at which it is common to find uncertainty about where digitally shared materials go (one-to-many social media platforms; search engine use; the inherent "leakiness" of machines); and finally, I reach a scale where workers are dealing with the meta-data of a population's economic activity (tax operations). With each movement comes a corresponding shift in the role played by art objects as conversation partners. Le Fraga's *W8ING* merely has to evoke the common experience of texting, while Claburn's/AOL user 23187425's *i feel better after i type to you* has to manifest the agency of information and its distribution through information machines and human users. Finally, Wallace's *The Pale King* grounds the abstraction of the info-sphere's totality. In whatever proportion necessary, aesthetic-affective speculation helps to close the gap between human perception and overload boredom – making visible something that is hidden by virtue of its size.

Using the vocabulary of spiritual resources found in historical boredom discourse, I have spoken through this carefully curated selection of art objects in order to cultivate an aesthetic-affective relationship with information overload. My reading of Sophia Le Fraga's *W8ING* in chapter 3 recognizes how texting instills the passage of time with rhythms, using waiting as a way to dial up or down social closeness and social distance. Placing texting in this frame supports an analysis of boredom and info-tech in ritual terms. I read Thomas Claburn and AOL user 23187425's *i feel better after i type to you* as a kind of confession that we offer up so much of ourselves as online information in order to be witnessed. This scenario links boredom and information, according to information theory, as a problem of meaning. A withdrawal from the realm of the private could mean reducing uncertainty about ourselves. Together, both scenarios reveal how our use of info-tech is not just compulsion and addiction, but also something intimate and *care*ful – habitual. Yet habitual cycles of info-tech is exactly how overload boredom masks itself from our noticing.

With this revelation in hand, the analyses of *W8ING* and *i feel better after i type to you* act as the pillars on which the reading of *The Pale King* rests. They build a foundation to read *The Pale King* as being about a particular kind of boredom – the spiritual crisis of overload boredom. This is because though *The Pale King* has so much to say about information overload, it is set in the '80s and does not speak directly to the info-tech that is ubiquitous today. Without the readings of *W8ING* and *i feel better after i type to you*, we might not see in *The Pale King* how the specific form of the information technology is incidental – cellphones, search engines, paper IRS forms – wherever there is information overload, there is overload boredom.

In *The Pale King* we find new ways of relating to information overload that, instead of perpetuating or being mystified by it, stop the withdrawal from world and self: to pay attention, not in a pop-psych way, but to see the sorting through information overload as a kēdic exercise; to deal with the dull and treat the crushing waves of boredom; to appreciate the strangeness of the media ecology as something worthy of imaginative speculation. This is a mode of kēdic enchantment where aesthetic-affective investments in information overload hedge against the double withdrawal of overload boredom.

READING THE BOOK BACKWARDS

Reading backwards from *The Pale King* allows us to see how the info-technic modes represented in w8ING and *i feel better after i type to you*, particularly texting and online searching, can both *remediate* the disaffects of overload boredom and perpetuate conditions of overload in the contemporary media ecology.

For example in w8ING, poet Sophia Le Fraga's digital characters – like preprogrammed chatbots – speak incessantly of the dull. Their text message conversation makes a running commentary on the meaninglessness of their texting. In w8ING the characters have a relationship of mutual commitment to a third party and an ambiguous relationship with each other. The timing and tone of their texting suggests a subtle way of arranging social closeness and distance among themselves. These characters who are waiting for  also present us with a sociality that is not just a human-human shared boredom; theirs is shared agent-agent. In other words, w8ING is showing us what it is like to feel bored *with* other agents, whether social or technical. One of them could have been an AI chatbot – it is less a conversation, more a staging of *shared entropy*. Thus, being bored *with* does not dispel or cover up boredom. Their sharing does not resolve boredom because the *with* requires an intimacy – a dwelling together in the boredom. Their texting is one of those parts of life that is and must be dull.

After recognizing the possibility of kēdic enchantment through *The Pale King*, a new logic of intimacy opens up for us. We can perceive that the logical consequence of being kēdically intimate with boredom is neither that we would stop texting nor feel compelled to reply, but rather that the experience of texting would be more *aesthetic* less *disaffective*. The more intimate you are with overload boredom as a sociohistorial context, the less your experience of texting is characterized by anxious waiting for reply on the one hand, and compulsion to send text messages on the other. Though the characters of w8ING are mystified, the performance Le Fraga stages them in expresses a kēdic aesthetic. If their texting is one of those parts of life that is and must be dull, then at least it has become art.

My reading of *i feel better after i type to you* conceptualized sharing personal information online as a sharing of uncertainty (entropy), which now we can read as an example of the mystifying potential of information overload. AOL user 23187425 writes incessantly about nothing much going on in their search queries in a way that materializes a real-life Fogle – a parrhesiac confessing to the search engine.

User 23187425's monologue was hidden by virtue of the size of the data leak in which it appeared. Their collective data entries over almost a month indicate a developing intimacy and meaning-making with the practice of digital searching. In a kēdic reading we recognize that user 23187425 was perhaps not mystified. In fact the kēdic nature of *i feel better after i type to you* is double, as Claburn's act of curation – his act of caring – is what gives us the visual history of why they (user 23187425) feel better after they type. It took Claburn combing through millions of lines of the accidentally released search engine results to sort the entropy and make it information by introducing it to a human social context as a "poem" capable of speaking of its own dullness.

The way these art objects use surplus information, or, information overload as their medium and message highlights the sensuousness of information, the tangibility of information technologies, and the social concreteness of how these things mediate human relationships. Reading them together shows how digital disturbance of time and meaning by too much information and choice is the disaffective texture of overload boredom.

* * *

The overarching argument of *The Spiritual Significance of Overload Boredom* – that boredom is structural and collective, as well as psychological and personal – hinges on the fact that information and choice are configured together in ways that belong to the age of overload. What emerges affectively from an age of overload are tendencies toward flattened affect, withdrawal from the world, and disorientation of time and meaning – overload boredom.

Hopefully, the foregoing has done something to equip us to choose where our attention goes, instead of letting the vast array of desire-engine-powered options take it. Instead of choices with no real alternatives, we have to make a real alternative. And that real alternative is to not withdraw. Not to settle in the loneliness and melancholy, even if we must accept it. As Thomas Dumm (2008, 23) writes in *Loneliness as a Way of Life*: "The inclination of modern life, with its distractions and shallowness, obscures the deeper fact of our separation from each other. So we need to establish a certain distance from our distractions in order to think more clearly about what it is we are seeking from each other. It is in the silence that we may come to recognize the fact of our ghostly existence, our fatal separation from each other, and from our better selves. And yet it is this separation that we must preserve so as to come to understand the dangers that accompany our ongoing attempts to overcome it." We cannot put a moratorium on info-production. What I propose we can do is absorb this heuristic outlook: at the scale of information overload in info-capitalist society, information behaves more like mere data by so often rendering us ignorant of its context by way of its speed and volume, from which we are liable to withdraw, producing the disaffective medium of overload boredom. If we can be affecognizant of this masking, we can see our information sharing practices in terms of sharing entropy – in terms of an attempt to reduce affecognitive entropy, and thereby increase our capacity for aesthetic-affective speculation on ourselves and other beings. Alive to this impulse, we are better equipped to make deliberate kēdic choices regarding overload boredom as a disaffective medium of the collective.

In the face of overload's tendency to make us withdraw, and therefore forget, remembering the history of boredom as a spiritual crisis with corresponding exercises of care is a source of hope to redefine our systems. This is more than a personal solution because my concept of overload boredom aims, as all philosophy does, to broadly reiterate the way a phenomenon shows up in the cultural imaginary. That is, if we can attune ourselves to noticing the psychological emotion of boredom, or the activity of texting, or the acceptance of unreadable reams of privacy terms and conditions as the tip of the iceberg of overload boredom, then we can perhaps gradually confront the withdrawal and forgetting that overload boredom produces to mask itself. This is the ethic to which kēdic hermeneutics gives rise.

As Whitney Bauman (2020, 7) writes of developing an ethic of "critical faith" after the Anthropocene: "speculation is precisely what helps us materialize different ways of becoming. We need different stories about possible beginnings and possible future becomings in order to break out of singular historical narratives. We need spectral thinking in order to discern the spectrum of possibilities." We need to listen to what the 24/7 Demon is trying to tell us about the spiritual significance of boredom if we are ever going to cease being mystified by overload. Because the overload of information today comes primarily via "new media," it has a way of sounding like a new problem – the screen addiction of youth; the less-than-twenty-four-hour news cycle; etc. But actually, these media and the way we use them are just the logical consequence of the teleology of capitalism as it moves from its industrial to informational form. Existential discontent arises when the work of subjectivization is troubled by the wrong relationship between information and meaning. Thinking the shared spiritual crisis of overload boredom allows us to perceive overload boredom as our era in the longue durée.

EPILOGUE

For Boredom

There is a companion website to *The Spiritual Significance of Overload Boredom* called *For Boredom: Conceptual Art and Writing on Boredom as a Crisis of Meaning*, which shifts focus from the argumentative mode of this book back to the art objects that are its backbone: http://forboredom.realtimecollective.com. On this site you will find excerpts of primary sources and secondary sources in a variety of media (text, drawing, film, etc.). They are annotated – and available to be annotated by you, the visitor – with a view to drawing links between concepts of boredom, spirituality, and information overload. These annotations also connect different works to each other, helping patterns emerge from the content of the sources and the content of the analysis of them (i.e., the annotations). In order to be included, a work has to meet two out of three criteria: boredom is thematized; spirituality is thematized; information overload and meaning-making are problematized by the structure of the work. For the purposes of the site, relevant are all instances where the stem "spirit" or "bor-" appears across different lexical forms (e.g., "spiritual," "spirituality," "spiritualize," etc.; "boring," "bored," "bore," etc.). They are treated as analytic categories whose possible meanings encompass their whole history of use in both emic and scholarly contexts. With the first two criteria set in relationship to the third one, "overload boredom-as-spiritual-crisis" becomes a heuristic for making sense of contemporary boredom that neither necessarily denigrates or celebrates technological, social, symbolic, and other elements of overload culture.

Each type of source – primary or secondary, scholarly or creative, textual or visual, or any blend thereof – is treated as worthy of annotation in its own right. This organization is modeled on Kenneth

Goldsmith's UbuWeb, a huge online archive of conceptual writing, avant-garde, ethnopoetics, and outsider arts. Prefacing UbuWeb are Goldsmith's "usual arguments against creativity and for copyleft, file-sharing, and free culture" (Goldsmith in Allen 2013), including his claim:

> For the moment, we have no competition, a fact we're not happy about. We're distressed that there is only one UbuWeb: why aren't there dozens like it? Looking at the art world, the problem appears to be a combination of an adherence to an old economy (one that is working very well with a booming market) and sense of trepidation, particularly in academic circles, where work on the internet is often not considered valid for academic credit. As long as the art world continues to prize economies of scarcity over those based on plentitude, the change will be a long time coming. But UbuWeb seeks to offer an alternative by invoking a gift economy of plentitude with a strong emphasis on global education. (Goldsmith 2011)

For Boredom modestly hopes to contribute, if not compete. With this online platform it is possible to dive deeper into an aesthetic-affective mode of engagement with the "overload boredom-as-spiritual-crisis" heuristic by enabling a certain kind of close reading. It is a reading concerned with how knowledge feels; a process involving the materiality of the text that, together with the embodiment of the digital interface and the reader, creates "registers of meaning that compel passions" (Schaefer 2018, 69). Specifically, *For Boredom* is fragmentary (given the format of the annotations), but therefore also infinitely and collaboratively expandable (well, to the point of certain technological limitations). In its own way, it is also increasingly dense and synthetic, owing to the functions of searching and hyperlinking. I hope you will enjoy and add to it.

As in this book, the website's focus on overload boredom-as-spiritual-crisis does not imply a normative claim that all instances of boredom are spiritually inflected, or that spirituality denotes some sui generis reality whose true nature we are trying to uncover. Instead, it offers a particular, sociohistorically grounded prompt for exploring dis/affective structures of contemporary existential anxieties and orientations. The website is about understanding problems of meaning that arise from diversions and manipulations of interest, attention, focus, etc., but in some senses, each is also "for" boredom in the way that Martin Jay (1996) was "for theory" (in the lineage of Alvin W. Gouldner who was "for sociology," via Louis Althusser who was "for Marx"): it advocates for the critical potential of overload boredom as a concept and as a disaffective medium that compels thinking|feeling about both.

Notes

PREFACE

1 In the only book yet to be written on the relationship between boredom and religion, *Boredom and the Religious Imagination* (1999), Michael Raposa takes a (Peircean) semiotic view of boredom as a failure of interpretation, an inability to read signs in life *as* meaningful.

2 I use this formulation of "mind|body," and later a compound formulation "thinking|feeling" in order to speak the simultaneity of sensational, experiential, and expressive processes always going on with human beings. There is no thinking without feeling, or vice versa, and there is no cognition without embodiment, because cognition evolved in part as an adaptive strategy for the survival of the organism's body. My use of mind|body, in particular, recalls the formulation of N. Katherine Hayles, whose conception of the linkage between human and machine bodies is important for my arguments about interior experience amid information overload which follow. In *Writing Machines*, Hayles calls the interface where user and machine interact the "mindbody" (2002, 48). This interaction "creates new connections between screen and eye, cursor and hand, computer coding and natural language … these connections perform human subjects who cannot be thought without the intelligent machines that produce us even as we produce them" (63). When I use the mind|body compound, I also recall the critical legacy of the concept "bodymind" in disability studies, which points out how the intertwinement of the mental and the physical is animated in particular ways in the context of (dis)ability, where our technologies may be barriers, prostheses, enhancements, etc. Scholars like Sami Schalk (e.g., in *Bodyminds Reimagined* 2018), show how race, gender, and other categories critically determine the nature of these intertwinements.

3 Having had some research experience in philosophy of cognitive science (Viger, Bluhm, and Mosurinjohn 2008), I was interested to discover some writers noting that cognitive neuroscience may support the connection between time and boredom: there is a brain region called the insula where it is suspected that the experience of emotions and temporal passage interface, and it is thought to be active in the feeling of boredom (Toohey 2011, 172–3).

4 Scholarly interest in boredom has been intensifying from a range of arts, humanities, and social sciences, especially in the past decade. There is now a nascent interdisciplinary theorization of how boredom has changed as an experience of everyday life in the twenty-first century. The groundbreaking multidisciplinary *Boredom Studies Reader: Frameworks and Perspectives* (Haladyn and Gardiner 2016) attests to this, consolidating on that ground a new field, however small. Elsewhere, for instance, cultural studies scholar Liam Mitchell (2013) has looked at boredom and aggression in online communities like 4Chan, while the composer and theorist Eldritch Priest has analyzed the aesthetics of boredom in sonic culture. Sociologist Michael E. Gardiner (2014) has examined the role of boredom in the latest incarnation of capitalism to dominate the globe, what he calls info-capitalism or semiocapitalism, and philosopher Mark Kingwell (2019b) has explored boredom and digital interfaces. Their analyses are astute, and I see the present book as extending shared terrain.

5 One of the iconic "instruction pieces" is the conceptualist John Baldessari's *I Will Not Make Any More Boring Art* (which appears in my penultimate chapter). This piece consists of the titular phrase written out over and over across the gallery walls in the manner of the classroom punishment of writing lines. Baldessari (2009) described conceptual art as throwing "a corral around your idea." His conceptual engagement with boredom belongs to a long succession of avant-gardes who have turned their boredom into art.

6 By "aestheticize" I do not mean make pretty, but rather make *sensible*.

7 In fact, in the earliest phase of my research, it was the concept of "interior experience" (Mosurinjohn 2014), not "boredom," that was the frame through which my research initially took place.

8 In 1986, the sociologist Orrin E. Klapp wrote *Overload and Boredom: Essays on the Quality of Life in the Information Society*, where he links boredom and information in the following way. Klapp contends that, if meaning and interest are found mostly in the mid-range between extremes of redundancy and variety, then boredom must be associated with the extremes of banality and noise. In a way, these extremes, redundancy

and chaos, collapse into each other. Redundancy is repetition of the same, which creates a condition of insufficient difference, while noise is the chaos of non-referentiality, or entropy. As such, boredom can be viewed "as a loss of potential ... for a certain line of action at least" (Klapp 1986, 3).

9 The concepts and scholarly categories that are central to this book – like boredom, religion and spirituality, information- and choice overload – are categories that belong to the modern, Western context. So far, I have spoken about my own experiences. But occasionally I will speak of experiential conditions that are shared. Whenever I speak of these conditions belonging to an "us," or a collective "you," I am referring to those whose lives are shaped by these categories and this context, to whatever extent that they are. I make no claims about "the human condition" generally, nor do I assume a static meaning for boredom and its relationship to religion, spirituality, and other existential forms. Nor do I assume that because a surfeit of choice exists in the "consumer-hell type situation" (Wallace [2005] 2009, 93) of a metropolitan grocery store, it exists everywhere, or even for everyone walking through that store. Purchasing power and access to information and social opportunities are significantly gendered and racialized as well as contextual to particular times and places. But the pressure to self-make and aspire to "more" is still present in them. I am interpellating you, the reader, to whatever extent and in whatever way this pressure bears on your life.

INTRODUCTION

1 At various points, I have reckoned with the claim of classicist Peter Toohey that "profound" or "existential" boredom is just "a hotchpotch of a category, and one whose basis is more intellectual than experiential" (2011, 6). I have therefore wondered whether another concept other than boredom could have helped me do my analytical work just as well, or better (my concern with arbitrariness abides). It struck me that akēdia (Greek; or acedia, Latin), perhaps the earliest link in the chain of boredom, arose with the early Christian monks who had isolated themselves in the desert, and there, their loneliness paired with their creeping anxiety that the particular supernatural worldview to which they had committed was, in the end, wrong. Loneliness and anxiety can certainly be thought of as component parts of boredom. Or, you could think of each term – boredom, anxiety, loneliness – as explaining parts of the other. You could think of loneliness as social boredom, for instance. You can be lonely because you have no companionship or you can be lonely in a relationship

because you fail to attend or to take interest – to care, and therefore to find it meaningful. Time fails to fly when you are not having fun. You could likewise describe boredom as a loneliness for things (you can be bored because you have nothing to do) or for the world at large (you can be bored when you have lots to do but you fail to attend to it). Surely loneliness has some component of existential dread about alienation of the self from itself, others, and the world, as does anxiety. Søren Kierkegaard, the "father of existentialism" – who wrote memorably on both boredom and anxiety – claimed that anxiety "is altogether different from fear and similar concepts that refer to something definite" (in Marino 2015). It seems to me that boredom is similarly "indefinite," in that it has to do with the nature of time, how to use it properly, and therefore how to dispose of human freedom, which can conjure the existential dread that this freedom means that no matter what we do, we might never legitimately and finally satisfy the need to feel meaning. But if you drill down into fear and similar concepts, as well as into emotions with the opposite valence, do they not all have to do with self and world, and how these two are distributed amongst each other? And if we try to imagine what is ultimately at stake in them, do they not all speak to some fundamental concern about the nature of existence? In the end, however, it is not my concern whether different forms of boredom are more intellectual or experiential. It is boredom's whole discursive history pertaining to ideas and experiences of time, information, choice, and existential meaning that made it my conceptual anchor.

2 I have in mind here Jacques Rancière's (2005) concept of "the distribution of the sensible." This is how Rancière names "the system of self-evident facts of sense perception that simultaneously discloses the existence of something in common and the delimitations that define the respective parts and positions within it" (2004, 12).

3 For one concise history, see the introductory essay by Barbara Dalle Pezze and Carlo Salzani (2009) in their edited volume *Essays on Boredom and Modernity*. In it, they claim that the English term "boredom" did not exist before the seventeenth century and they perform a genealogy of some of the terms that came before it – acedia, melancholy, ennui, spleen, *Langeweile* [German, "long while"] – concluding that modern boredom is "a recent and different phenomenon" (Dalle Pezze and Salzani 2009, 5).

4 Of course, cultural speed is not brand new. Speed was a hallmark of Fordist-era modernity. Yet today, the targets and means of acceleration have clearly changed. For a classic treatment of speed and culture, see Paul Virilio's ([1977] 1986) *Speed and Politics: An Essay on Dromology*, which considers the logic and effects of speed as the foundation of

technological society. For a recent discussion of speed with a political programme for dealing with the cultural conditions of capitalist technology, see Steven Shaviro's (2015) *No Speed Limit: Three Essays on Accelerationism*. Shaviro proposes we push capitalist technologies to the point where they "explode." It is also worth noting, however, how popular culture is beginning to reject its own obsession with speed, including a number of various "slow" movements spawned off of Italy's slow food movement that aimed to counter the culture of fast food. The problem of speed has captured writers of non-fiction popular work like James Gleick in *Faster: The Acceleration of Just about Everything* (1999) and Daniel Kahneman in *Thinking Fast and Slow* (2011). Likewise, it has absorbed novelists like Abha Dawesar, who is preoccupied by the drive to virtually connect in what she calls "the digital now," and Milan Kundera (1995, 2), who writes in *Slowness* that "speed is the form of ecstasy that humanity has been given by the technical revolution." Writers involved with media, information, and technology studies implicitly work with the notion of acceleration in merely describing the technological conditions of information transfer.

5 Another treatment of contemporary boredom in relation to new media specifically is Mark Kingwell's work, including "Bored, Addicted, or Both: How We Use Social Media Now" (2016), and *Wish I Were Here: Boredom and the Interface* (2019).

6 I coin the term "habritual" as a portmanteau of "habit" and "ritual."

7 I am talking about aspects of what Gilles Deleuze (1992) called "societies of control." Societies of control are no longer restrained by "environments of enclosure" like the prison, hospital, family, school, or factory (Deleuze 1992, 3–4).

8 Berardi (2011) develops info-capitalism from Jean Baudrillard's concept of semiocapitalism, which first connected the critique of capitalism to semiotics. See also Gardiner (2014), on boredom and semiocapitalism, specifically.

9 "Western" here is serving as a heuristic for speaking to the broad and rangy influence of Western Europe as it gets mediated and transformed in a North American context without actually reifying or affirming a static culture or identity.

10 One mode of which Jonathan Beller (2016) calls "informatic labour," which is where "the digital image itself exploits the attentive labor of those who see it, organizes profitable patterns of spectatorship, and links communication directly to financial speculation." He links this to Walter Benjamin's observation that "by means of aestheticization and the

preservation/re-invention of ritual (cult) values … the masses are granted 'not their right but instead a chance to represent themselves.'"

11 In the context of "everyday aesthetics" aesthetics is a method (to analyze something as one would an art object) and an adjective (a modifier of "experience"). That experience might be of an everyday thing, the experience of which takes us out of the everyday. Or we might take an everyday experience and analyze it aesthetically. But it is an open question whether we are any longer talking about aesthetics when we are talking about *ordinary* experiences of everyday things. Thomas Leddy, one of the central figures in everyday aesthetics, has written that "it would seem we need to make some distinction between the aesthetics of everyday life ordinarily experienced and extraordinarily experienced. However, any attempt to increase the aesthetic intensity of our ordinary everyday life-experiences will tend to push those experiences in the direction of the extraordinary. One can only conclude that there is a tension within the very concept of the aesthetics of everyday life" (2005, 18).

12 Here I follow the work of contemporary religious studies scholars who are investigating the practices people consider spiritual (e.g., Bender 2010), and charting the ways they make things special (e.g., Taves 2009). I am especially indebted to the work of Ann Taves in *Religious Experience Reconsidered: A Building-Block Approach to the Study of Religion and Other Special Things* (2009) and Gordon Lynch in *The Sacred in the Modern World: A Cultural Sociological Approach* (2012) on the making of second order terms. These thinkers have showed that in spite of terms like "the spiritual" and "the sacred" coming under sustained attack for presupposing some theological referent, if we do not assume that some of our objects are inherently religious and others not, then our object of study becomes things that share a stipulated point of analogy as they intersect with case sites where claims about the value, meaning, and significance of things and experience are inchoate and/or contested (I am paraphrasing closely, and in order, from: Lynch 2012, 15; Taves 2009, 25; Taves 2010, 318).

13 There is a body of neo-Marxist and ideology critiques of spirituality as a bourgeois form of personal religion that capitalism sells to reproduce itself. Examples include Jeremy Carrette and Richard King's *Selling Spirituality: The Silent Takeover of Religion* (2004), Craig Martin's *Capitalizing Religion: Ideology and the Opiate of the Bourgeoisie* (2014), and Véronique Altglas's *From Yoga to Kabbalah: Religious Exoticism and the Logics of Bricolage* (2014). Their argument that spirituality can function as an ideological veil to inequality in late modern societies is an

important part of the scholarly conversation about how "spirituality" functions among people who self-identify as spiritual (for a critique, see Mosurinjohn and Watts 2021). It should be clear at this point, however, that I am not talking about "spirituality" in their sense in this book. My project here picks up the language of "spiritual crisis" from the boredom theories of modern artists and scholars, and uses it as a heuristic for interpreting the disaffects of info-tech-driven culture in relation to the existential discontents expressed through historical boredom discourse.

14 Actually, the quotation is "so banal that in some ways we deserve to die" (Kripal 2020).

15 Speculative realism (SR) refers to a variety of philosophical positions engaged in some way with the problem that, since Immanuel Kant introduced a distinction in his 1781 *Critique of Pure Reason* between the noumenal (the world as it is "in-itself") and the phenomenal (the world as it appears to humans), philosophy has "stopped being occupied with reality" (Dolphijn 2016). The common ground of these different anti-correlationist positions is their refusal to reduce everything to what is "given to any consciousness or language" (Gratton 2014, 44). And different they are. There are many disagreements within various modes of speculative philosophy, one of which is between those who were participants in the 2007 conference at Goldsmiths, University of London, which marks an originary moment for SR. In grappling with whether SR can be said to constitute a "movement," the introduction to Peter Gratton's book notes that one of them, Ray Brassier, rejects the idea and the "agenda" of those who promote the idea that there is one. His statement that it "exists only in the imaginations of a group of bloggers" (in Gratton 2014, 2) is a reference to the fact that a lot of the debate goes on through the personal blogs of, especially, the object-oriented set, like Levi Bryant, Ian Bogost, and Graham Harman. These blog-based conversations can become rather insulated from the normal circuits of academic critique, even as they may also be more open to different online audiences.

16 For an inventive take on the "new-" or "neo-materialism" that has come from feminism, philosophy, science studies, and cultural theory, see *New Materialism: Interviews & Cartographies*, edited by Rick Dolphijn and Iris van der Tuin (2012). This volume offers discussions with four different leading lights (Rosi Braidotti, Manuel DeLanda, Karen Barad, and Quentin Meillasoux). In the first half, these scholars discuss how their work rereads older texts against the grain, while in the second half the editors situate the major questions of the interviewees with respect to broader contemporary thought. It is especially valuable for considering

how and why we might include certain work under the rubric of (new) materialism. I also note that it is important to contextualize new materialism with respect to the closely related "posthumanism." Posthumanism reimagines the concept of the "human" as embodied in ecological relation to other beings, whether biological life, artificial life, or nonlife, in the context of info- (semio-; cognitive-) capitalism (Mosurinjohn 2021). Some writers have identified one as a subset of the other, or vice versa, while others have characterized them as close, but distinct.

CHAPTER ONE

1 The connection between boredom and art has endured since the time of boredom's precursor concepts. In antiquity, since "acedia was a marginal phenomenon" available to those with spiritual and material privilege, there was "a certain cultural prejudice" that established "a connection between *acedia* and art" (Dalle Pezze and Salzani 2009, 8). In the Middle Ages the same connection could be seen, for instance, in Dante, who believed that "a certain sensuality within monotony can give birth to a hauntingly lovely song whose seductive melody can paralize [sic] the listener and prevent him from ever reaching home" (Reinhard Kuhn [1976] quoted in Dalle Pezze and Salzani 2009, 8). In modernity, when culture came to be dominated by the spectacle (a social relationship between people that is mediated by images [Debord (1967) 1983]) the concept of boredom instead became an animating force for the early avant-garde and especially the mid-century Situationist International, in attacking "consumption of the spectacle as product, which society provides as the bored subject's main antidote" (Haladyn 2008, 7). Art has continued to feed itself on boredom into the twenty-first century, as boredom spread beyond "the creative few" (Goodstein 2005, 174), helping to loose "the psychological and physical desire or energy of the subject that is blocked by everyday life" (Haladyn 2008, 6).

2 In boredom literature, both "acedia" (Latin) and "akēdia" (Greek) sometimes appear. Unless I am quoting or referring to an author who has used "acedia," I stick to "akēdia" for reasons that will become apparent later in the book (notably, chapter 5).

3 For a full exposition of the existential significance of boredom in Heidegger see Slaby (2010).

4 According to Alexandre Brierre de Boismont, "as a substitute for faith in a divine purpose, the commitment to work has become an end in itself" (in Goodstein 2005, 134). Unsatisfying ends begat unsatisfying ends.

This was part of a related set of reasons Brierre de Boismont chronicled in the article "De L'Ennui (Taedium Vitae)" for ennui as a "disease of civilization" which was found to be a factor in 237 of the suicides of his contemporaries out of the 4,595 cases examined. This finding contributed to tension in the modern discourse of boredom between metaphysical, sociological, and physiological causes.

5 Of course, we have now moved past the idea that religion is disappearing in the face of modern ideological pluralism and we acknowledge that modernity is enchanted in many of its own ways (e.g., Saler 2006; 2012; 2013; Landy and Saler 2009; Josephson-Storm 2017).

6 Consonant with the general German Jewish literary milieu of which Benjamin was a part, he was interested in tradition and storytelling. Benjamin was not, however, engaging boredom from the situation of Judaism's traditional practices of continual commentary on texts.

7 For Benjamin, boredom was both the "atrophy of experience" and "the dream bird that hatches the egg of experience" ([1936] 1969, 91). It is in the latter sense that boredom has revolutionary potential. Some moments of modern boredom are full of potential because they contain frustrated desires for something more. This kind of boredom is important "because it represents what he calls (in *The Arcades Project*) a 'Trojan horse,' by which a gradual mode of awakening can stealthily enter our commodified dreamworld and transform it into dialectical possibility" (Gardiner 2012, 53). Benjamin's fullest analysis of boredom appears in convolute "D" of the *Arcades Project* ("Boredom, Eternal Return") (1999).

8 Goodstein emphasizes boredom as a historical phenomenon rather than a human condition. She argues that some foundational boredom writers have erred toward the latter. For example, she notes that Reinhard Kuhn, in his 1976 *The Demon of Noontide: Ennui in Western Literature* construes ennui in Goethe and Chateaubriand "as an effect of the inherent insufficiency of earthly existence in the face of human longing for transcendence" (Goodstein 2005, 45). Each, she says, belongs to a subjectivity proper to different sides of the French Revolution (Goethe pre and Chateaubriand post).

9 This phrase is from the comedian Bo Burnham in his 2021 special *Inside*, where he sings in a song called "Welcome to the Internet": "Could I interest you in everything? / All of the time? / A little bit of everything / All of the time / Apathy's a tragedy and boredom is a crime / Anything and everything, all of the time."

10 I have in mind two literary moments here. The first is in Kierkegaard's *Either/Or*, where the aesthete describes boredom as follows: "Boredom rests upon the nothing that interlaces existence; its dizziness is infinite,

like that which comes from looking down into a bottomless abyss" ([1843] 1988, 291). The second is in the preface to Baudelaire's 1964 *Fleurs du Mal,* a poem called "To the Reader" (*Au Lecteur*):

Our sins are insistent, our repentings are limp;
We pay ourselves richly for our admissions,
And we gaily go once more on the filthy path
Believing that by cheap fears we shall wash away all our sins.
On the pillow of evil it is Satan Trismegistus
Who soothes a long while our bewitched mind,
...
In the infamous menagerie of our vices,
There is one uglier, wickeder, more shameless!
Although he makes no large gestures nor loud cries
He willingly would make rubbish of the earth
And with a yawn swallow the world;
He is Ennui! – His eye filled with an unwished-for tear,
He dreams of scaffolds while puffing at his hookah.
You know him, reader, this exquisite monster,
– Hypocrite reader, – my likeness, – my brother!

Ennui, descendent of akēdia and precursor to boredom, arises from "the triumph the individual has in making existence uninteresting" according to translator Eli Siegel (1968, 177). Siegel goes on to write: "This defeat of existence by individual non-responsiveness or individual incomplete participation is effectively related to all the other evils. Disrespect of what is not the self can lead to injustice to any aspect of that tremendous living and inanimate territory which is not oneself" (177).

11 My experience of working on this project to date shows me that there are readers inclined to critique it for not giving not enough specificity to the framing and justification for the experience and context I am examining here; and at the same time there are readers inclined to critique this project for spending too much time on the voices of others and lines of thought that acknowledge what is beyond the scope of the project – and therefore specify the phenomena under examination, but without advancing my own argument. While citation can be a feminist practice by which "we acknowledge our debt to those who came before; those who helped us find our way when the way was obscured because we deviated from the paths we were told to follow" (Ahmed 2017, 17), the requirement to engage the literature can prevent engagement with the proper boredom of reading one thing at great length and thinking one's own thoughts about it, especially for scholars whose own thoughts

are likely to be taken as less serious than others due to identity markers such as youth and female gender.

CHAPTER TWO

1 Bauman's term is "liquid modern culture," where "liquid" emphasizes change and temporariness. Throughout this book, I will most often speak of "info-capitalist culture" in order to emphasize the role of information technologies on human affect and cognition.

2 M. Gail Hamner (2018a) coined the term "affecognitive," which "posits that all cognition embeds affect ... If in today's world of intensifying social media and media prosthetics, the social comes to biological bodies predominantly through visual and sound images, the fabric of social life – biological, technological, institutional, and temporal – requires the actions and reactions of affecognitive circuits to generate, sustain, and (also) interrupt social consensus." I employ it here because it is an elegant concept for indicating the personal and collective nature of overload boredom, and its inextricability from media technologies (film being Hamner's focus) and the experiences they produce.

3 There are a great many other inspirations for my way of thinking here, including, especially, Ian Bogost (2012) and Don Idhe (2009). Bogost is a practicing video game designer trained in comparative literature. In his "alien phenomenology," he endorses a "panexperientialism," which takes the fact that all objects interact with others to entail that all things can be said to perceive and experience one another. The mechanisms through which they do this just may not be the ones human beings privilege in their attempts to grasp objects. For Bogost (2012, 6), this approach is a way of "drawing attention to things at all scales ... and pondering their nature and relations with one another and with ourselves." Idhe, on the other hand, endorses a "postphenomenology." In *Postphenomenology and Technoscience* Idhe defines the concept as a "nonsubjectivistic and interrelational phenomenology" that "short-circuits the 'subject/object' detour derived from Descartes ... and points much more directly to something like a lifeworld analysis" (2009, 11) of a being in its environment.

CHAPTER THREE

1 W.J.T. Mitchell has an interesting discussion of making visual sense of digital information in his chapter "Realism and the Digital Image" (2015). He describes the problem arising from digital art being too perfect. Our eyes

cannot process the perfection of the digital image, and so we see computer generated images as "fake." Contemporary digital film has had to come up with techniques for "dumbing-down" the image so we see it as "real."

2 Of course, this is not the first time that people have been using abbreviated asynchronous text; telegraphy being one important example. Linguist John McWhorter observes that spoken language is more "telegraphic" than written language, which it predates by tens of thousands of years. This leads him to argue that texting isn't written language, it's "fingered speech" (see Copeland 2013). Or maybe, less awkwardly, speech materialized visually instead of sonically.

3 In some of the laboratory and field research into choice, scientists have described the optimal set size as "reasonably large, but not ecologically unusual" (Iyengar and Lepper 2000, 996). Six is often what they use as a psychologically manageable number of choices, at least for consumer choice. In a consumer choice scenario, a psychologically excessive number of choices can be as little as twenty-four.

4 And especially the more letter-like medium of emailing; see Young 2014.

5 I will restrain myself from straying into the territory already so well-trodden by literature on the ever-expanding "mindfulness" movement. Mindfulness in its moves from East to West is comprehensively explored in Jeff Wilson's (2014) *Mindful America: The Mutual Transformation of Buddhist Meditation and American Culture*.

6 As Leo Tolstoy put it in *Anna Karenina* ([1877] 2000, 529).

7 It is hard to nail down precisely how many text messages are being sent and received or how much time people spend texting because different kinds of messaging are tracked differently (app messages are sent via WiFi, while SMS messages are sent via cellular signals), and texting behaviours vary by demographic. However, what is clear is that texting is a global phenomenon. Phones are the primary messaging device globally (Twilio 2016).

8 On the topic of fragmentation, see: Nasaw 1993; hooks 1995; and Ashby 2006.

9 What is most commonly referred to by the noun "text" is actually the "Short Message Service" message, typically capped at 160 characters.

10 The sense of "careful performance of ritual obligations" survives from Roman antiquity "in the English adverbial construction 'religiously' designating a conscientious repetitive action such as 'She reads the morning newspaper religiously'" (Smith 1998, 269–70).

11 This is not new, exactly, to *social* media. In *Overload and Boredom* Orrin E. Klapp (1986, 6) wrote: "A media system delivers far more and different

information, from strangers outside, than does an oral system, from members inside. Soon it becomes a system in which life is geared to media – in which people literally get up and go to bed by media; they are media-oriented: plugged into telephone, television, radio, cassettes, computers, film, credit-card transactions, and all the rest most of the time, on the job, in their cars, on the way to and from work, and at home. They hustle to keep up with information. Media orientation becomes a dependency that some experts do not hesitate to call addiction." Klapp's emphasis on *dependency* is another viable angle on the relation of overload boredom, media, and addiction in addition to those I have emphasized above.

12 The way our networking technologies also polarize, divide, monetize, distract, control, and manipulate us is explored in the 2020 drama-documentary hybrid *The Social Dilemma*.

13 A nascent literature on digital hoarding further attests to this desire (see Chen 2014; Falkoff 2017), though the existence of ephemeral messaging attests to its risks.

14 After observing how soldiers of the Great War continued to relive their trauma in the form of "shell shock" and other anxieties Freud was compelled to amend his concept of the "pleasure principle" (*eros*) with the counterbalancing proposition of the death drive (*thanatos*). It was clear to him that people not only instinctively seek self-preservation but that they also act on an instinct that "paradoxically tends to self-annihilation through self-conservation" (Woltersdorff 2012, 133). What needed explaining was "the compulsion of the human psyche to repeat traumatic events over and over again" (Felluga 2011).

15 Though the two happen to have a deep relation – there is a dictum that war is 1 per cent terror and 99 per cent boredom (Laugesen 2012).

16 Liam Mitchell (2013) even ups the ante on this notion by proposing that the troll tackles the "desire for desires" problem by erecting "a conscious barrier to unconscious desire" by eliding investment in its principal object, which is amusement at another's expense, or "lulz." In Mattathias Schwartz's (2008) formulation, lulz is "a quasi-thermodynamic exchange between the sensitive and the cruel"; humour derived from "disrupting another's emotional equilibrium." In pursuing lulz, the troll establishes "a distance from other trolls (with whom he may or may not feel a bond) and from the people who are governed by normal formations of desire" (Mitchell 2013). Insofar as the troll's pursuits "bypass or forestall normal formations of desire, they may be characterized as non-subjective." This is significant because, as Mitchell says, our choices only "have lasting

meaning, for others and for ourselves ... when we can be held accountable to our promises," and this is impossible in a condition of both online anonymity and refusal of subjectivity. There are many ways that, as said in *Les Fleurs du Mal* (1857, xxv), "ennui makes your soul cruel."

CHAPTER FOUR

1 Fittingly, AOL user 23187425 is listed as the author of this work on the Lulu.com website where it is for sale as a print-on-demand book. (In a further gesture of care for the plight of user 23187425, Claburn donates half of the profit from each copy of the book sold to the Electronic Frontier Foundation, which defends people's digital rights). But only Claburn is listed as the author in the excerpt reproduced in Goldsmith and Dworkin's anthology of "uncreative" conceptual writing *Against Expression* (2011). The way I discuss *i feel better after i type to you* in this chapter acknowledges the collaboration of both people, and their machines.

2 Although Goldsmith describes constraint-based writing as a "poetics of the moment" – that moment being the information age – he acknowledges that projects like the ones he and Craig Dworkin collected in the *Against Expression* anthology have strong roots in the mid-century era of conceptualism. One of the major forces that emerged in this era is something known as Oulipo – *Ouvroir de Litterature Potentielle* [Workshop of Potential Literature]. Oulipo was founded by French mathematician Francois de Lionnais and writer Raymond Queneau in 1960 with a playful vision of generating endless outcomes through the application of a system of structural constraints to existing poems and as a way of creating new ones. Oulipians are still meeting and writing today.

3 Canonical examples include Goldsmith's own books like *Day* (2003), where over the course of one year he retyped verbatim every scrap of text visible to him in one issue of the *New York Times*, and *Fidget* (2000), which attempts to report an exhaustive account of his own actions on one day, but unfolds instead an infinite metacognitive regress that shows the impossibility of lossless representation. Works like these confront information overload with "obsessive archiving and cataloging" (Goldsmith 2008). My next chapter explores the formal logics, aesthetic values, and affective outcomes of this antiexpressive strategy.

4 According to Klapp, the sociological consensus on this problem had once been that of William Ogburn (1922) and Stuart Chapin (1928), who argued that material culture (like digital media technology) changes faster than

nonmaterial culture (like beliefs, relations, affects), resulting in cultural maladjustment to material realities, and therefore, in social problems. Klapp (1982) instead retrieves the notion of "lag" to express it in terms of a relationship between these two kinds of information.

5 Information is not infinitely fast, though. Information is fundamentally material, and is therefore subject to constraints. The Shannon-Hartley Theorem states that with an increase in the information rate that can be transmitted over a given bandwidth in a communication system ("spectral efficiency"), there is an increase in power required. More power is required because there are more bits being moved *and* because each bit actually requires more power to move. Because of this, there is a bound on the maximum amount of error-free information per time unit that can be transmitted within a specified bandwidth in the presence of noise interference.

6 Klapp lists "poverty of ritual" as another factor that narrows the bottleneck, presumably because ritual creates meaning by arranging information in a shared framework and by consolidating it via repetition. Ritual may be impoverished with respect to the info-sphere, but habritual is abundant.

7 Humans are not the only ones doing the measuring, since ontologically speaking, humans, dice, scientific laboratories, and the concept of uncertainty are all objects with some (and different) degrees of independence, agency, and experience of their own. The making of information depends upon the agency of the human "receiver" and the humans and technologies that are "senders," as well as the information itself that can either behave disruptively and "get in its own way" by drowning out a desired signal, or else "act" like communication by balancing parameters such as loudness, rate, amount, repetition, encryption, (lack of) feedback, and contextuality. Recently the scientist and philosopher Karen Barad has developed an ontology of "agential realism," holding that apparently "'distinct' agencies are only distinct in a relational, not an absolute, sense, that is, agencies … don't exist as individual elements" (33). What Barad calls the "intra-action" of these agencies performs an "agential cut" to mark out such boundaries around apparent individuals. In other words, "things" are not a precondition of relations; phenomena constitute things, which do not exist outside of those phenomena. Barad's performative account of material bodies (both human and nonhuman) pose a hard challenge to realism. Agential realism advances the generative and unsettling idea "that distinct agencies do not precede, but rather emerge through" mutual entanglement, collaboration (Barad 2007, 33).

8 Information (or the lack thereof) is defined mathematically in terms of the *logarithm* of the number of unknown states. The logarithm is the exponent of the power to which a base number must be raised to equal a given number. The simplest example given by Adami is that of tossing a fair six-sided die. Your uncertainty about the state of this die before throwing it is log 6. Say you toss it and it lands with the number five up. When you look at the number that came up (that is to say, when you make your measurement), you have reduced your uncertainty (about the outcome of this throw) to zero. You know exactly what state the system has taken on in terms of the way you parameterized the possibilities of the system, based on what you wanted to know and the measurement devices available to you. But this gets more complex when you consider conditional probability distributions. In the case that we know something about the system, then the equation can be written $I = H(X) - H(X \mid Y)$. We can read this as: information is "the difference between the actual observed entropy of X, minus the actual observed entropy of X given that I know the state of Y (whatever that state may be)" (Adami 2016, 12).

9 Responding to a hypothetical reader, Adami writes: "Information is shared entropy. 'Shared information' would be, like, shared shared entropy. I think that's a bit ridiculous, don't you think?" (2016, 11).

10 Presencing is surely not the *only* way of relating to the affordances, lures, and demands of the online world. Artist and critic Hito Steyerl (2012) makes a startling observation about how much actual people have disappeared from the "dark matters of the digital world," only to be replaced with photochopped avatars, or what she calls "Image Spam." In her essay "The Spam of the Earth: Withdrawal from Representation," she writes: "dense clusters of radio waves leave our planet every second. Our letters and snapshots, intimate and official communications, TV broadcasts and text messages drift away from earth in rings, a tectonic architecture of the desires and fears of our times" (Steyerl 2012). All these images floating around the globe, "desperately vying for human attention" (Steyerl 2012) make time feel scarce. "Warhol's prediction that everybody would be world-famous for fifteen minutes had become true long ago. Now many people want the contrary: to be invisible, if only for fifteen minutes. Even fifteen seconds would be great" (Steyerl 2012). Steyerl's own iconoclastic practice, like the videos *Strike* and *Strike II*, see her literally taking hammers to screens, effacing the author, effacing the art, effacing the audience.

11 At one point, Adami writes: "if I have been using the words 'entropy' and 'uncertainty' interchangeably, then I did this on purpose because they are one and the same thing here. You should use one or the other

interchangeably too. But you should never say 'information' when you do not know what you can predict with the entropy at hand." This raises the question: is it really personal *information* that's at stake and *information* surveillance that many denizens of the info-sphere are concerned about? What does Adami mean about knowing what you can predict? Information and entropy are parasitic concepts, but information also depends on antecedent information. Adami says "an unconditional entropy must be maximal: it tells us how much we do not know if we do not know anything except how many states my measurement device has." But he also says "everything is conditional." For any system, once you acquire any information about the states, we then know that some states are going to be more likely than others. So if you have your measurement device, you how how many states it has, and if you are measuring something, "you already come equipped with some information about the system you are interested in (built into your common sense)" – by virtue of being a thing that *experiences*, you cannot help but already know something about whatever system you're measuring, and that means that you necessarily know something about what you can predict with the entropy at hand, so yes, it is information. The state of knowing absolutely nothing about what you can predict with the entropy at hand can only exist as a thought experiment. Information, therefore, is the condition of matter – "a dynamism immanent to bodily matter and matter generally," as affect theorist Patricia Clough (2010, 207) says.

12 Giroux (2014) goes on to say that "in the current period of historical amnesia, privacy has been redefined through the material and ideological registers of a neoliberal order in which the right to privacy has succumbed to the seductions of a narcissistic culture." But this is maybe overstated – all of humankind is invested with destructive traits like narcissism in different concentrations. It merely has more frequent and visible outlets.

13 In 2006, as now, AOL search was powered by Google, which uses natural language processing based on machine learning. Specifically, it uses statistical language models that encode information about how language is used. This information is learned from the web by looking at billions of web pages. The search spell checker, for instance, would evaluate AOL user 23187425's line "could have gone to detriot" by suggesting corrections for "detriot" and evaluate these suggestions in the context of the phrase in order to determine the likeliest candidate for what the user actually meant to type. If we imagine Claburn retyping or at least editing a litany of anonymous curiosities and statements, we might wonder whether he was tempted to answer or suggest better-formed questions and propositions, as we might be tempted to do, and as browsers and SMS

software are increasingly tempted to do with "autocomplete" suggestions. As they accumulate, en masse certain patterns in our search queries materialize; the evolution of computer programming languages used in database management systems and in search engines is toward recognizing these patterns. But instead of spellchecking and search results, in Claburn's piece the response to this litany is almost total silence.

14 "Nonconscious and unconscious actions" are "powerful sources of cognition" (Hayles 2012, 95). Sensory processing works at around 11 million bits per second, most of which, about 10 million bits per second, streams through in vision. Consciousness is far slower. Reading in your head, for instance, happens at about 45 bits per second. "In other words, consciousness can only deal with a very small percentage of all incoming information. All the rest is processed without awareness" (Dijksterhuis, Aarts, Smith 2005, 82) – about 200,000 times as much. Facts like these reveal the machinic in the human, bringing human agency into question, and highlighting how cognition is shared by both biological and nonbiological beings.

15 Schaefer now prefers the word "recalcitrance." In a 2016 interview he said: "I thought about [the choice of the word 'intransigence'] a lot after I published the book. I'm not sure that intransigence was the right word to use in that chapter. The word that I really wanted was *recalcitrance*. Recalcitrance literally means 'it kicks back.' [Affect has] got a punch of its own, its own ability to insert itself into a dynamic field. It has a push. With intransigence, I had in mind the image of something that is refusing to budge, rather than a concrete wall. Because I don't think that affects are like a concrete wall, but I do think that they kick back. They have the ability to push themselves into subjectivity in a way that needs to be taken seriously, both in their biological, psychological profiles, as well as in their ability to concretely reconfigure systems of power."

CHAPTER FIVE

1 For a deeper dive into the political dimensions of *The Pale King*, see Clare (2012), "The Politics of Boredom and the Boredom of Politics in David Foster Wallace's *The Pale King*."

2 There is a slipperiness involved in talking about *The Pale King* as book, "David Wallace" as narrator of it, and David Foster Wallace as an author of this and other works, at different moments throughout this chapter. I am not making a case for authorial intent necessarily in everything I say about *The Pale King*. Rather, Wallace the author, Wallace the narrator,

and *The Pale King* itself all become characters within this chapter, with their own kinds of agency.

3 Whereas the setting of *Infinite Jest* in the near future allows Wallace to project out hilarious and catastrophic consequences of the digital revolution, *The Pale King* takes place when it is just underway. My sense is that it is linked to the fact that in the 1980s bureaucrats and office workers had the communicative limitations of fairly primitive computers (by today's standards) plus the unpredictable, backlogging inefficiencies of physically transporting information on paper. The scenario puts one in mind of the much earlier pronouncement by the founder of cybernetics Norbert Wiener. Expressing a vision both globally expansive and somehow hauntingly narrow, in 1948 Wiener wrote: "for man [sic], being alive means the same thing as participating in a broad global system of communication" (in The Invisible Committee 2014, 3). Wallace's world certainly feels hermetically sealed in this way; life for his characters is almost completely coextensive with the IRS system.

4 Wallace has a number of characters slip in this in-group/out-group distinction that it is only lay people who call it "the IRS," while insiders say "the service."

5 Some scenes in *The Pale King* consist of characters responding to non-diegetic questions in the manner of a reality TV "confessional," or a quasi-legal interrogation, or, in some cases, the ritual of disclosing truth to a spiritual director. There also echoes here of the description of AOL user 23187425 (see Dworkin and Goldsmith 2011, 138).

6 An antiexpressive writer like Goldsmith, for example, would take an enabling constraint – say, recording every movement his body made in a day (*Fidget*) – and write hundreds of dull pages about it. And Jacques Roubaud, a member of Oulipo, summarised the conceptual art axiom developed with the mid-century avant-garde this way: "a text written according to a constraint describes the constraint" (1998, 42).

7 Surrealists, who adopted the term "automatism" from psychology and psychiatry, hoped to express the creative force of a unique psyche through writing and drawing in a trance state. Citational "antiexpressive" work is precisely against expressing a subjectivity in this way. Rather it could be said that citational work instantiates subjectivization in moments of choice. As Goldsmith (2011, 203) says of an assignment where he asked students to retype a piece of text they found, "in the act of retyping" one "thing that differentiates one student from another is the choice of *what* to retype." Other questions arise: "what did your choice of paper stock say about you: your aesthetic, economic, social, political, and environmental

circumstances?" (203). In psychology, automatism is where behaviour and consciousness are supposed to be dissociated from one another. Automatism can either be the result of "familiarity and long usage" which allows "actions to become automatic so that they are performed with a minimum of thought and deliberation," or it can be "pathological" (Gibson 2009). Pathological automatism may ensue from "psychological conflict, drugs or trance states" (Gibson 2009). Contemporary citation instead implies what might be called "'the new unconscious' (or 'adaptive unconscious')," which "plays a critical role in understanding" the way "attention comes into play as a focusing action that codetermines what we call materiality" (Hayles 2012, 14). When, through rules of selection and recursion, it mirrors "the structured forms of relational databases and database queries" (16), it also mirrors new views that "the unconscious does not exist primarily as repressed or suppressed material but rather as a perceptive capacity that catches the abundant overflow too varied, rich, and deep to make it through the bottleneck of attention" (14). Rather than externalizing that which issues from an interior subjectivity, citational poetics performs an embodied acknowledgement of the way perceptual filters that used to protect us from the data flowing from the outside in are ineffective against the ways we have found to increase bandwidth of the data coming in. It is a form of appropriation significantly transformed by the application of rules which themselves transform the work, and, if concerned with originality and cycles of consumption as c. 1980s appropriation was, says the most about authoring hyperreality and managing overproduction.

8 Wallace was clearly aware, and critical, of the tradition of conceptual art and its dealings with boredom. He agrees with the conceptualists' critique of capitalist culture, but opposes their coldness and abstraction, insisting on sincerity and caring in his art. In fact *Infinite Jest* ruthlessly skewers the high postmodern conceptual artist and ghostly paterfamilias, James O. Incandenza for his cold, abstract, conceptual films. (I thank an anonymous peer reviewer for this wording.) One of which is a gesture to conceptual musician John Cage's *4:33*. Yet, to be fair to the antiexpressivists, their work should not be caricatured as being all about cool irony. Their work is not merely an attack on meaning or on audiences looking for it. This was the accusation Jo Baer made about minimalism in her caustic essay "I Am No Longer an Abstract Artist" (1983, 136).

9 The works which spawned Goldsmith's idea of the "unboring boring" (2004) only revealed their insights about boredom in the process of *making* them. There is nothing you learn about Goldsmith's retyping of an issue of the *New York Times* by actually reading every word of

either the original or his retyping. The process of making is where a concept instantiates all kinds of particular and unpredictable problem-solving, which comes to constitute the detail and specificity of the work. But literary critic and longtime interlocutor of Goldsmith Marjorie Perloff (2010) suggests that maybe we ought not to take Goldsmith at face value when he says it doesn't matter whether or not we read his work.

10 For instance, the mid-twentieth century "instruction pieces" of artists like Sol LeWitt, John Baldessari, and Yoko Ono registered the idea of an artwork in a set of instructions for making it. Since it did not have to be made, it did not have to be consumed.

11 After all, according to Sol LeWitt (1967, 83), "conceptual art is good only when the idea is good."

12 Considering AOL user 23187425's treatment of the search box for "confession" (or perhaps prayer), Claburn wonders "what circumstances prompted the author to converse thus with AOL's search engine" (in Dworkin and Goldsmith 2011, 138).

13 For which, of course, he is sometimes disliked and/or dismissed. One reviewer wrote: "Much as J.D. Salinger increasingly felt his work should promote his belief in Vedantic and Buddhist beliefs, there's something unnervingly zealous about the way the novel addresses the perennial DFW concern of how to be a good person in a world full of aggravation, solipsism and distractions. Well and good, but the people who achieve some kind of meditative transcendence – adjusting themselves to concentrating on banality for hours on end – can be annoying, pedantic and nearly-Asperger's in their inability to empathize" (Rizov 2011).

14 The book essentially uses a Skinnerian intermittent reinforcement schedule by providing small rewards of action, drama, and beauty, punctuated by large tracts of dullness.

15 Adam S. Miller (2016, 77) says with respect to *The Pale King* and Wallace's other long works like the >1000-page *Infinite Jest*, "boredom is a head-clearing ascesis." By this he means it looks like, feels like, is like monastic endurance. But Miller fails to unpack the meaning of ascesis as both the feeling of boredom and the doing of spiritual exercises, collapsing the meaning, feeling, and doing, of boredom – in other words, collapsing the phenomenological experience of boredom and the behaviour it calls for in response. Boredom (akēdia) requires the spiritual exercises of ascesis to resolve the boredom into an experience of peace. The practice of reading is what does the head-clearing, but only insofar as it is interpreted as a practice of care – what we will soon see is called "kēdia" – for self and other. It is kēdia that resolves the akēdia.

16 Wallace wrote "every love story is a ghost story." I say: every boredom story is a demon story.

17 Dean learns that his boredom is part of a history of struggle related to work and the unavailability of energy for doing meaningful work (entropy). When the noontide demon attacked monks "in the stillness of the midday hour and emptie[d] the world of any meaning," the existential disorientation was only temporary (Dalle, Pezze, and Salzani 2009, 8); ultimately, their meaning was secured because they laboured in an ontology that placed them under the surveillance – literally, the watching from above – of God. Not so for Lane Dean and his compatriots labouring under the watchful eye of the clock. In the twenty-first century, the drives of consumer culture have steadily overtaken the principle of the holiness of everyday work that had been affirmed from Benedict to the Protestant Reformation. What remains for Dean and his coworkers is the ideology of economic wealth as an end in itself and an autocratic management theory that has yielded organizational techniques such as the "open office panopticon" to replace the watchful eye of God (Benefiel, Fry, and Geigle 2014, 176). But in other scenarios and with other characters, *The Pale King* also shows office work reinvested with the spiritual significance of boredom that was conceived before capitalist alienation. This reinvestment takes place through the practice of askesis. What Dean's demon coyly leaves leaves out of his word history is the spiritual exercises that were bundled with the pathos of boredom in the meaning of ἀκηδία.

18 This could be thought of on the model described by psychologist of religion Matt Rossano (2013) in his book *Mortal Rituals*, in which technology is conceptualized as being about controlling the environment enough to bend it to our advantage, and ritual being about finding the inner resources to keep on keeping on.

19 If something is deadly boring, but has legal, financial, and, ultimately, social and psychic ramifications, then both failures of attention and failures of design are at stake. Legal scholar Art Cockfield (2015) considers this problem in relation to the very real phenomenon of workplace boredom in the business of tax law in his article "David Foster Wallace on Tax Policy, How to Be an Adult, and Other Mysteries of the Universe." In Cockfield's view, "*The Pale King* is saying that it's possible to get past the monotony. We can choose to look at the workday, not as some dreary horror, but as an adventure." In a more satirical mood, the graphic novelist Robert Sikoryak considers the same sort of problem through his *Terms and Conditions* (2017). *Terms and Conditions* reproduces Apple's legal contract for the iTunes app verbatim, illustrating each page in the style

of a different famous comic artist and depicting Steve Jobs as the protagonist. Its newfound readability is a one-off solution to dense legal text, letting it serve more, as one reviewer put it, "as a surreal record of our modern digital age in which the rules for our tools have become Bible-length, and just as sacred" (Heller 2017).

20 For more on enchantment and spirituality, see Mosurinjohn and Watts (2021), which makes a theoretical discussion of the way cultural sociological approaches – and I add here philosophical approaches – to the study of spirituality can take seriously the notion that discourses and practices of spirituality express desires for enchantment and (potentially) supra-empirical frameworks of meaning without taking a stance on whether the alleged sources of enchantment actually exist.

21 In my treatment of enchantment, I follow Jane Bennett, as mentioned in chapter 3. While mystifying enchantment contributes to the spiritual crisis of overload boredom, kēdic enchantment soothes it.

22 The truth of this is apparent in large-scale intelligence enterprises and in microsociology of surveillance workers. While bulk data collection may be seductive to governments and other institutions directing the collection, the opacity of the data to those seeing it close up can prove frustrating. The journalist Julia Angwin (2013) reports that "in March 2013, some NSA analysts asked for permission to collect less data through a program called Muscular because the 'relatively small intelligence value it contains does not justify the sheer volume of collection.'" This was according to a document leaked by Edward Snowden. Meanwhile at the time of Angwin's writing, the NSA was having to build a new storage center in Utah designed "to hold more than 100,000 times as much as the contents of printed materials in the Library of Congress." As Snowden himself has said (in a statement through his lawyer): "When your working process every morning starts with poking around a haystack of seven billion innocent lives, you're going to miss things" (in Angwin 2013). The reasons for this are simultaneously logistical and affective.

23 Fogle could be read more charitably as parrhesiac than logorrheic. According to the list of exercises that have come down to us from antiquity including "self-research, investigation (skepsis), reading, freedom of speech (parrhēsia), and attentiveness (prosochē). This latter refers to a kind of vigilance of mind and self-consciousness. It includes concentration on the present moment and the examination of dreams. Here we see an intimate connection between presence to others and presence to oneself. For every spiritual exercise is a dialogue and the interlocutor is extremely important, even if at times the dialogue becomes a combat. What counts

is not the solution but the process [play; equifinality]. It is here that the subject forms her or his thought" (Hadot 1987). Parrhēsia "refers to the need to conceal nothing of what one thinks but rather to speak in complete openness to one's 'guide'" (Allouch 2014).

24 The moment can be found on page 191: "And yet these flickers of deeper awareness, whether drug-induced or not – for it is arguable how much that ultimately matters – probably had more of a direct effect on my life and direction's change and my entering the Service in 1979 than did my father's accident, or possibly even more than the dramatic experience I underwent in the Advanced Tax review class that I had sat in on by mistake during my second, ultimately much more focused and successful enrollment at DePaul" (Wallace 2011, 191).

25 A post-book note says: "A note from chapter 22 suggests that Chris Fogle knows a string of numbers that when recited give him the power of total concentration. But nowhere in the chapter does Fogle display this power" (Wallace 2011, 541). And later: "Point is to extract from Chris Fogle the formula of numbers that permits total concentration? Point is he can't remember – he wasn't paying attention when he happened to read the series of documents that added up to the string of numbers that, when held in serial in his head, allows him to maintain interest and concentration at will? Has to be sort of tricked into it? Numbers have downside of incredible headache" (543).

26 For another take on boredom as religious experience in Wallace's *The Pale King*, see Sheehan 2011.

27 People experience Fogle as strange because he both makes them bored and models a way of relating to that boredom. He is a synecdoche for *The Pale King*, as boredom was a "synecdoche for the spiritual crisis of modernity" (Goodstein 2005, 224).

28 Risov's (2011) reason being that "one of the feats of Wallace's prose is that it renders not only palatable but fresh potentially tired bromides."

References

Abolfazli, Maryam. 2014. "Are We Dating? And Other Confusions Created by Texting." *Medium*. 27 June. https://medium.com/@maryack/are-we-datingand-other-confusions-created-by-texting-7a577b730994.

Adami, Christoph. 2016. "What is Information?" *Philosophical Transactions of the Royal Society* A374: 1–14. 13 March. http://dx.doi.org/10.1098/rsta.2015.0230.

Ahmed, Sara. 2006. *Queer Phenomenology: Orientations, Objects, Others*. Durham: Duke University Press.

– 2017. *Living A Feminist Life*. Durham: Duke University Press.

Albrechtslund, Anders. 2008. "Online Social Networking as Participatory Surveillance." *First Monday* 13, no. 3. 3 March. http://firstmonday.org/article/view/2142/1949.

Allen, Mark. 2013. "Proudly Fraudulent: An Interview with MOMA's First Poet Laureate, Kenneth Goldsmith." *The Awl*. February 6. https://www.theawl.com/2013/02/proudly-fraudulent-an-interview-with-momas-first-poet-laureate-kenneth-goldsmith.

Allouch, Jean. 2014. "Fragilités de L'Analyse." *Critique*: 1–12.

Altglas, Véronique. 2014. *From Yoga to Kabbalah: Religious Exoticism and the Logics of Bricolage*. Oxford: Oxford University Press.

Althusser, Louis. 2006. *Philosophy of the Encounter: Later Writings, 1978–87*. Edited by François Matheron and Oliver Corpet. Translated by G.M. Goshgarian. New York: Verso.

Anderson, Ben. 2004. "Time-Stilled Space-Slowed: How Boredom Matters." *Geoforum* 35, no. 6: 739–54.

Andrejevic, Mark. 2013. *Infoglut: How Too Much Information is Changing the Way We Think and Know*. New York: Routledge.

Angwin, Julia. 2013. "NSA Struggles to Make Sense of Flood of Surveillance Data." *Wall Street Journal*, 25 December. http://www.wsj.com/articles/SB10001424052702304202204579252022823658850.

Arata, Emily. 2014. "The Mid-Typing Texting Bubble Is Actually Causing People Severe Anxiety." *Elite Daily*, 5 September. http://elitedaily.com/news/technology/typing-bubbles-iphones-cause-texting-anxiety/742398.

Arendt, Hannah. 1958. *The Human Condition*. Chicago: University of Chicago Press

Arrington, Michael. 2006. "AOL Proudly Releases Massive Amounts of Private Data." *TechCrunch*, 6 August. https://techcrunch.com/2006/08/06/aol-proudly-releases-massive-amounts-of-user-search-data.

Ashby, Leroy. 2006. *With Amusement for All: A History of American Popular Culture since the 1830s*. Lexington: The University Press of Kentucky.

Auerbach, David. 2014. "I Built That 'So-and-So Is Typing' Feature in Chat." *Slate*, 14 February. http://www.slate.com/articles/technology/bitwise/2014/02/typing_indicator_in_chat_i_built_it_and_i_m_not_sorry.html.

Baird, Benjamin, Jonathan Smallwood, Michael Mrazek, and Julia W.Y. Kam. 2012. "Inspired by Distraction: Mind Wandering Facilitates Creative Incubation." *Psychological Science* 23, no. 10: 1117–22.

Baldessari, John. 2009. "Systems." *PBS*, 10 September. http://blog.art21.org/2009/09/10/meet-the-season-5-artist-john-baldessari.

Barad, Karen. 2007. *Meeting the Universe Halfway: Quantum Physics and the Entanglement of Matter and Meaning*. Durham: Duke University Press.

Bar-Anan, Yoav, Timothy D. Wilson, and Daniel T. Gilbert. 2009. "The Feeling of Uncertainty Intensifies Affective Reactions." *Emotion* 9, no. 1: 123–7.

Baudelaire, Charles. 1857. *Les Fleurs du Mal*. French versions and English translations from the 1857, 1861, 1866, and 1868 publications prepared by Supervert with special reference to the translations of Edna St Vincent Millay. Accessed 30 May 2014. http://fleursdumal.org.

Baudrillard, Jean. (1968) 2005. *The System of Objects*. London: Verso.

Bauman, Whitney. 2020. "Returning Faith to Knowledge: Earthlings after the Anthropocene." *Religions* 11, no. 169: 1–10. http://doi.org/10.3390/rel11040169.

Bauman, Zygmunt. 2008. *Does Ethics Have a Chance in a World of Consumers?* Cambridge: Harvard University Press.

Beckett, Samuel. (1953) 1982. *Waiting for Godot: Tragicomedy in 2 Acts*. New York: Grove Press.

Beller, Jonathan. 2016. "Informatic Labor in the Age of Computational Capital." *Lateral* 5, no. 1. https://doi.org/10.25158/L5.1.4.

Bender, Courtney, and Ann Taves, eds. 2012. *What Matters?: Ethnographies of Value in a Not So Secular Age*. New York: Columbia University Press.

Benefiel, Margaret, Louis W. Fry, and David Geigle. 2014. "Spirituality and Religion in the Workplace: History, Theory, and Research." *Psychology of Religion and Spirituality* 6, no. 3: 175–87.

Benjamin, Walter. (1936) 1969. "The Storyteller: Reflections on the Work of Nikolai Leskov." In *Illuminations*, edited by Hannah Arendt, 83–110. New York: Schocken Books.

– 1999. *The Arcades Project*. Translated by Howard Eiland and Kevin McLaughlin. Cambridge, MA, and London: The Belknap Press.

Bennett, Jane. 2001. *The Enchantment of Modern Life: Attachments, Crossings, and Ethics*. Princeton: Princeton University Press.

– 2010. *Vibrant Matter: A Political Ecology of Things*. Durham: Duke University Press

– 2012. "Systems and Things: A Response to Graham Harman and Timothy Morton." *New Literary History* 43: 225–33.

Bennett, Jessica. 2014. "Texting Anxiety Caused by Little Bubbles." *New York Times*, 29 August. http://www.nytimes.com/2014/08/31/fashion/texting-anxiety-caused-by-little-bubbles.html.

Berardi, Franco. 2011. "Time, Acceleration, and Violence." *e-flux* 27 (September). https://www.e-flux.com/journal/27/67999/time-acceleration-and-violence.

Berger, Peter L. 1979. *The Heretical Imperative: Contemporary Possibilities of Religious Affirmation*. New York: Anchor Press.

Biceaga, Victor. 2006. "Temporality and Boredom." *Continental Philosophy Review* 39: 135–53

Blas, Zach. 2016. "Understanding Queer Technological Strategy." *Gay Bombs*. Accessed 8 June 2018. http://users.design.ucla.edu/~zblas/thesis_website/gay_bombs/gb_part2.html.

Bogost, Ian. 2012. *Alien Phenomenology, Or, What It's Like to be a Thing*. Minneapolis: University of Minnesota Press.

Bosker, Bianca. 2011. "Americans Admit Using Their Phones to Avoid Others." *Huffington Post*, 16 August. https://www.huffpost.com/entry/how-americans-use-their-phone_n_928438.

Boswell, Marshall. 2012. "Trickle-Down Citizenship: Taxes and Civic Responsibility in David Foster Wallace's *The Pale King*." *Studies in the Novel* 44, no. 4: 464–79.

Brautigan, Richard. 1967. *All Watched Over by Machines of Loving Grace*. San Francisco: The Communication Company.

Brody, Richard. 2014. "Why Does It Matter if Heidegger Was Anti-Semitic?" *New Yorker*, 27 March. https://www.newyorker.com/culture/richard-brody/why-does-it-matter-if-heidegger-was-anti-semitic.

Bryant, Levi. 2013. "Politics and Speculative Realism." *Speculations* IV: 5–21.

Buck-Morss, Susan. 1992. "Aesthetics and Anaesthetics: Walter Benjamin's Artwork Essay Reconsidered." *October* 62: 3–41.

Burke, Kenneth. 2018. "How Many Texts Do People Send Every Day?" *Text Request*. Accessed 20 January 2021. https://www.textrequest.com/blog/how-many-texts-people-send-per-day.

Burnham, Bo. 2021. *Inside*. https://www.netflix.com/title/81289483.

Carey, James. (1988) 1992. *Communication as Culture: Essays on Media and Society*. New York: Routledge.

Carrette, Jeremy, and Richard King. 2005. *Selling Spirituality: The Silent Takeover of Religion*. New York: Routledge.

Castells, Manuel. 2004. "Informationalism and the Network Society." In *The Network Society: A Cross-Cultural Perspective*, edited by Manuel Castells, 3–45. Cheltenham: Edward Elgar Publishing Limited.

Chapin, F. Stuart. 1928. *Cultural Change*. New York: Century.

Chen, Anna. 2014. "Disorder: Vocabularies of Hoarding in Personal Digital Archiving Practices." *Archivaria* 78: 115–34.

Chun, Wendy. 2014. "Habitual New Media: The Involuntary, the Irrational and the Irresistible." NYU Media, Culture, Communication, April 24. http://vimeo.com/92835421.

– 2016. *Updating to Remain the Same: Habitual New Media*. Cambridge: MIT Press.

Chun, Wendy, and Sarah Friedland. 2015. "Habits of Leaking: Of Sluts and Network Cards." *differences: A Journal of Feminist Cultural Studies* 26, no. 2: 1–28.

Ciaunica, Anna. 2018. "When the Self Slips." *Aeon*, 21 June. https://aeon.co/essays/what-can-depersonalisation-disorder-say-about-the-self.

Claburn, Thomas, and AOL user 23187425. 2006. *i feel better after i type to you*. Superbunker.

Clare, Ralph. 2012. "The Politics of Boredom and the Boredom of Politics in David Foster Wallace's *The Pale King*." *Studies in the Novel* 44, no. 4: 428–46.

Clough, Patricia T. 2010. "The Affective Turn: Political Economy, Biomedia, and Bodies." In *The Affect Theory Reader*, edited by Melissa Gregg and Gregory J. Seigworth, 206–25. Durham: Duke University Press.

Cockfield, Art. 2015. "David Foster Wallace on Tax Policy, How to Be an Adult, and Other Mysteries of the Universe." *Pittsburgh Tax Review* 12: 89–109. http://doi.org/10.5195/taxreview.2015.35.

Collins, Graham P. 2002. "Claude E. Shannon: Founder of Information Theory." *Scientific American*, 14 October. https://www.scientificamerican.com/article/claude-e-shannon-founder.

Copeland, Michael V. 2013. "Texting Isn't Writing, It's Fingered Speech." *Wired*, 1 March. https://www.wired.com/2013/03/texting-isnt-writing-its-fingered-speech.

Crain, Cæmeron. 2013. "Living in A Society of Control." *Mantle*. Accessed 17 October 2020. https://www.themantle.com/philosophy/living-society-control.

Crair, Ben. 2014. "I Can See You Typing." *New Republic*, 21 January. http://www.newrepublic.com/article/116268/gchat-typing-indicator-most-awkwardfeature-online-chat.

Crystal, David. 2008. "Texting." *ELT Journal* 62, no. 1: 77–83.

Current, The. 2018. "Under the Knife and Unaware? What Happens When We're Under Anesthesia." *CBC*, 25 June. https://www.cbc.ca/radio/thecurrent/the-current-for-june-25-2018-1.4720521/under-the-knife-and-unaware-what-happens-when-we-re-under-anesthesia-1.4720542.

Dalle Pezze, Barbara, and Carlo Salzani, eds. 2009. *Essays on Boredom and Modernity*. Amsterdam: Rodopi.

Dawesar, Abha. 2013. "Life in the 'Digital Now.'" TEDTalk, June. http://www.ted.com/talks/abha_dawesar_life_in_the_digital_now.

Debord, Guy. (1967) 1983. *Society of the Spectacle*. Translated by Ken Knabb. London: Aldgate Press.

Deleuze, Gilles. 1992. "Postscript on the Societies of Control." *October* 59: 3–7.

Derrida, Jacques. 1987. *Of Spirit: Heidegger and the Question*. Paris: Galilee.

– 1995. *Archive Fever: A Freudian Impression*. Translated by Eric Prenowitz. Chicago: University of Chicago Press.

Dijksterhuis, Ap, Henk Aarts, and Pamela K. Smith. 2005. "The Power of the Subliminal: Subliminal Persuasion and Other Potential Applications." In *The New Unconscious*, edited by Ran R. Hassin, James S. Uleman, and John A. Bargh, 77–106. Oxford: Oxford University Press.

Dolphijn, Rick. 2016. "Review of *Speculative Realism: Problems and Prospects*, by Peter Gratton." *Notre Dame Philosophical Reviews*, 29 March. https://ndpr.nd.edu/news/speculative-realism-problems-and-prospects.

Dolphijn, Rick, and Iris van der Tuin, eds. 2012. *New Materialism: Interviews & Cartographies*. Ann Arbor: Open Humanities Press.

Dominus, Susan. 2015. "Motherhood, Screened Off." *New York Times Magazine*, 24 September. https://www.nytimes.com/2015/09/24/magazine/motherhood-screened-off.html.

Dumm, Thomas. 2008. *Loneliness as a Way of Life*. Cambridge: Harvard University Press.

Dworkin, Craig. 2011. "The Fate of Echo." In *Against Expression: An Anthology of Conceptual Writing*, edited by Craig Dworkin and Kenneth Goldsmith, xxiii–liv. Evanston: Northwestern University Press.

Dworkin, Craig, and Kenneth Goldsmith, eds. 2011. *Against Expression: An Anthology of Conceptual Writing*. Evanston: Northwestern University Press.

Eliot, T.S. 1934. "The Rock." New York: Harcourt, Brace, and Company.

Elliott, Carl. 2004. *Better Than Well: American Medicine Meets the American Dream*. New York: W.W. Norton & Co.

Ellis, Darren, Ian Tucker, and David Harper. 2013. "The Affective Atmospheres of Surveillance." *Theory and Psychology* 23, no. 6: 716–31.

Evagrius Ponticus. 1981. *The Praktikos. Chapters on Prayer*. Translated by J.E. Bamberger. Kalamazoo, MI: Cistercian Publications.

Eyal, Nir. 2012. "Want to Hook Your Users? Drive Them Crazy." *TechCrunch*, 25 March. http://techcrunch.com/2012/03/25/want-to-hook-your-users-drive-them-crazy.

Falkoff, Rebecca. 2017. "An Introduction to Hoarding." *Discard Studies: Social Studies of Waste, Pollution & Externalities*, 2 March. https://discardstudies.com/2017/03/02/an-introduction-to-hoarding.

Faye, Emmanuel. 2009. *Heidegger: The Introduction of Nazism into Philosophy in Light of the Unpublished Seminars of 1933–1935*. Translated by Michael B. Smith. New Haven: Yale University Press.

Felluga, Dino. 2011. "Modules on Freud: Transference and Trauma." *Introductory Guide to Critical Theory*. Purdue University. Accessed 26 May 2015. http://www.purdue.edu/guidetotheory/psychoanalysis/freud5.html.

Fish, Stanley. 2018. "Stop Trying to Sell the Humanities." *Chronicle of Higher Education*.

Freud, Sigmund. (1920, 1930) 1995. *The Standard Edition of the Complete Psychological Works of Sigmund Freud*. 24 vols. Edited by James Strachey, Anna Freud, Alix Strachey, Alan Tyson, and Angela Richards. London: Hogarth Press and the Institute of Psycho-analysis.

Friedan, Betty. 1963. *The Feminine Mystique*. New York: W.W. Norton & Company, Inc.

Gale, John. 2017. "Ἀκηδία and the 'Care of the Self.'" *European Journal of Psychoanalysis* (10 April). https://www.journal-psychoanalysis.eu/ἀκηδία-and-the-care-of-the-self-a-contribution-to-the-study-of-the-relationship-between-the-tradition-of-spiritual-exercises-and-psychoanalysis.

Gardiner, Michael E. 2012. "Henri Lefebvre and the 'Sociology of Boredom.'" *Theory, Culture & Society* 29, no. 2: 37–62.

– 2014. "The Multitude Strikes Back?: Boredom in an Age of Semiocapitalism." *New Formations* 82: 29–46.

– 2016. "Postscript: Not Your Father's Boredom: *Ennui* in the Age of 'Generation Meh.'" In *The Boredom Studies Reader: Frameworks and Perspectives*, edited by Julian Jason Haladyn and Michael E. Gardiner, 234–46. New York: Routledge.

Gibson, Jennifer. 2003. "Automatism." *Grove Art Online*. Oxford University Press. Published online 12 August 2019. http://www.oxfordartonline.com/subscriber/article/grove/art/T005221.

Giroux, Henry A. 2014. "Totalitarian Paranoia in the Post-Orwellian Surveillance State." *Truthout*, 10 February. https://truthout.org/articles/totalitarian-paranoia-in-the-post-orwellian-surveillance-state.

Gleick, James. 1999. *Faster: The Acceleration of Just about Everything*. London: Little Brown.

Goffman, Erving. 1967. *Interaction Ritual: Essays in Face-to-Face Behavior*. Chicago: Aldine Publishing Company.

Goldenberg, Naomi. 2013. "Theorizing Religions as Vestigial States in Relation to Gender and Law: Three Cases." *Journal of Feminist Studies in Religion* 29, no. 1: 39–52.

Goldsmith, Kenneth. 2000. *Fidget*. Toronto: Coach House Books. http://archives.chbooks.com/online_books/fidget/text.html.

– 2003. *Day*. Great Barrington: The Figures.

– 2004. "Being Boring." Delivered at Red Cat Symposium. Accessed 5 March 2015. http://epc.buffalo.edu/authors/goldsmith/goldsmith_boring.html.

– 2008. "Conceptual Poetics." *Harriet: Blog of the Poetry Foundation of America*. Accessed 6 March 2015. http://poetryfoundation.org/harriet/2008/06/conceptual-poeticskenneth-goldsmith.

– 2011. "Resources." Accessed 13 January 2015. *UbuWeb*. http://www.ubu.com/resources.

Goodstein, Elizabeth. 2005. *Experience without Qualities: Boredom and Modernity*. Stanford: Stanford University Press.

Gratton, Peter. 2014. *Speculative Realism: Problems and Prospects*. New York: Bloomsbury Academic.

Hadot, Pierre. 1987. *Exercices Spirituels et Philosophie Antique*. Paris: Études Augustiniennes.

Haladyn, Julian Jason. 2015. *Boredom and Art: Passions of the Will to Boredom*. Washington: Zero Books.

Hall, Stuart. (1973) 2007. "Encoding, Decoding." In *The Cultural Studies Reader*, edited by Simon During, 477–87. 3rd edition. New York: Routledge.

Hamner, M. Gail. 2018a. "Affect Theory as a Tool for Examining Religion Documentaries." In *Feeling Religion*, edited by John Corrigan, 93–116. Durham: Duke University Press.

– 2018b. "What is 'Affecognitive'?" *Affecognitive: Religion, Film, Affect, Academia* (11 April). https://affecognitive.wordpress.com/2018/04/11/what-is-affecognitive.

Hand, Martin. 2016. "#Boredom: Technology, Acceleration, and Connected Presence in the Social Media Age." In *The Boredom Studies Reader: Frameworks and Perspectives*, edited by Julian Jason Haladyn and Michael E. Gardiner, 115–29. New York: Routledge.

Harari, Yuval. 2017. *Homo Deus: A Brief History of Tomorrow*. London: Harvill Secker.

Harman, Graham. 2010a. "Meillasoux's Spectrum." *Object-Oriented Philosophy* (10 June). https://doctorzamalek2.wordpress.com/2010/06/10/meillassouxs-spectrum.

– 2010b. "Time, Space, Essence, and Eidos: A New Theory of Causation." *Cosmos and History: The Journal of Natural and Social Philosophy* 6, no. 1 (9 November). https://www.cosmosandhistory.org/index.php/journal/article/view/133.

Hayles, N. Katherine. 2002. *Writing Machines*. Cambridge, MA: MIT Press.

– 2012. *How We Think: Digital Media and Contemporary Technogenesis*. Chicago: University of Chicago Press.

– 2014. "Speculative Aesthetics and Object-Oriented Inquiry (OOI)." *Speculations: A Journal of Speculative Realism* V: 159–79.

– 2017. *Unthought: The Power of the Cognitive Nonconscious*. Chicago: University of Chicago Press.

Heidegger, Martin. (1929–30) 1995. *The Fundamental Concepts of Metaphysics: World, Finitude, Solitude*. Translated by William McNeill and Nicholas Walker. Bloomington: Indiana University Press.

Heller, Steven. 2017. "You Will Obey." *Print*, 22 February. http://www.printmag.com/daily-heller/terms-and-conditions-graphic-novel.

hooks, bell. 1995. "Postmodern Blackness." In *The Truth about the Truth: De-confusing and Re-constructing the Postmodern World*, edited by W. Truett Anderson, 117–24. New York: Penguin Putnam.

Hutson, Matthew. 2014. "People Prefer Electric Shocks to Being Alone with Their Thoughts." *Atlantic*, 3 July. https://www.theatlantic.com/health/archive/2014/07/people-prefer-electric-shocks-to-being-alone-with-their-thoughts/373936.

Idhe, Don. 2009. *Postphenomenology and Technoscience: The Peking University Lectures*. New York: SUNY Press.

Invisible Committee, The. 2015. *To Our Friends*. Translated by Robert Hurley. Cambridge, MA: MIT Press.

Iyengar, Sheena S., and Mark R. Lepper. 1999. "Rethinking the Value of Choice: A Cultural Perspective on Intrinsic Motivation." *Journal of Personality and Social Psychology* 76, no. 3: 349–66.

James, William. 1977. *The Writings of William James: A Comprehensive Edition*. Edited by John J. McDermott. Chicago: University of Chicago Press.

Jay, Martin. 1996. "For Theory." *Theory and Society* 25, no. 2: 167–83.

Josephson Storm, Jason. 2017. *The Myth of Disenchantment: Magic, Modernity, and the Birth of the Human Sciences*. Chicago: University of Chicago Press.

Kahneman, Daniel. 2011. *Thinking, Fast and Slow*. New York: Lane.

Kant, Immanuel. (1781) 1998. *Critique of Pure Reason*. Translated and edited by Paul Guyer and Allen W. Wood. Cambridge: Cambridge University Press.

Katz, James. 2003. "Bodies, Machines and Communication Contexts: What is to Become of Us?" In *Machines That Become Us: The Social Context of Personal Communication Technology*, edited by James Katz, 311–20. New Brunswick: Transaction.

Kepler, Johannes. (1604) 2000. *Optics: Paralipomena to Witelo & Optical Part of Astronomy*. Translated by William Donahue. Santa Fe: Green Lion Press.

Key and Peele. 2018. "Text Message Confusion." *Comedy Central*. https://www.youtube.com/watch?v=XaIB3NUxCMQ.

Kierkegaard, Søren. (1843) 1959. *Either/Or*. Vol. 2. Translated by David F. Swenson, Lillian Marvin Swenson, and Walter Lowrie. Garden City: Doubleday.

– (1843) 1988. *Kierkegaard's Writing, III, Part I Either/Or*. Edited and translated by Howard V. Hong and Edna H. Hong. Princeton: Princeton University Press.

Kingwell, Mark. 2016. "Bored, Addicted, or Both: How We Use Social Media Now." In *Social Media and Your Brain*, edited by Carlos Prado, 15–37. Santa Barbara, CA: Praeger.

– 2019a. "Why Being Bored Is Good." *Walrus*, 3 December. https://thewalrus.ca/why-being-bored-is-good.

– 2019b. *Wish I Were Here: Boredom and the Interface*. Montreal and Kingston: McGill-Queen's University Press.

Klapp, Orrin E. 1982. "Meaning Lag in the Information Society." *Journal of Communication* 32, no. 2: 56–66.

– 1986. *Overload and Boredom: Essays on the Quality of Life in the Information Society*. Westport: Greenwood Publishing Group Inc.

– 1991. *Inflation of Symbols: Loss of Values in American Culture*. Piscataway, NJ: Transaction Publishers.

Kotsko, Adam. 2018. *Neoliberalism's Demons: On the Political Theology of Late Capital*. Stanford: Stanford University Press.

Kripal, Jeffrey. 2019. *The Flip: Epiphanies of Mind and the Future of Knowledge*. New York: Bellevue Literary Press.

– 2020. "The Flip: Epiphanies of Mind and the Future of Knowledge." *New Books in Religion Podcast*. https://podcasts.apple.com/us/podcast/jeffrey-j-kripal-flip-epiphanies-mind-future-knowledge/id426502373?i=1000487883819.

Kuhn, Reinhard. 1976. *The Demon of Noontide: Ennui in Western Literature*. Princeton: Princeton University Press.

Kundera, Milan. 1996. *Slowness: A Novel*. Translated by Linda Asher. New York: HarperCollins.

Landy, Joshua, and Michael T. Saler, eds. 2009. *The Re-Enchantment of the World: Secular Magic in a Rational Age*. Stanford: Stanford University Press.

Latour, Bruno. 2005. "'Thou Shall Not Freeze-Frame,' or, How Not to Misunderstand the Science and Religion Debate." In *Science, Religion, and the Human Experience*, edited by James D. Proctor, 27–46. Oxford: Oxford University Press.

Laugesen, Amanda. 2012. *"Boredom is the Enemy": The Intellectual and Imaginative Lives of Australian Soldiers in the Great War and Beyond*. Surrey: Ashgate.

Le Fraga, Sophia. 2014. *W8ING*. Gauss PDF. 21 January. http://www.gauss-pdf.com/post/74187485516/gpdf093-sophia-le-fraga-w8ing.

Leddy, Thomas. 2005. "The Nature of Everyday Aesthetics." In *The Aesthetics of Everyday Life*, edited by Andrew Light and Jonathan M. Smith, 3–22. New York: Columbia University Press.

Lefebvre, Henri. (1947) 1991. *Critique of Everyday Life*. Vol. 1. Translated by John Moore. London: Verso.

– (1961) 2002. *Critique of Everyday Life*. Vol. 2. *Foundations for a Sociology of the Everyday*. Translated by John Moore. London: Verso.

– (1981) 2005. *Critique of Everyday Life*. Vol. 3. *From Modernity to Modernism*. Translated by Gregory Elliott. London: Verso.

Legge, Elizabeth. 2016. "Boring Cool People: Some Cases of British Boredom." In *The Boredom Studies Reader: Frameworks and Perspectives*, edited by Julian Jason Haladyn and Michael Gardiner, 81–98. New York: Routledge.

Levitin, Daniel. 2014. *The Organized Mind: Thinking Straight in the Age of Information Overload*. New York: Dutton.

– 2015. "Why the Modern World Is Bad for Your Brain." *Guardian*, 18 January. https://www.theguardian.com/science/2015/jan/18/modern-world-bad-for-brain-daniel-j-levitin-organized-mind-information-overload.

Licoppe, Christian. 2004. "'Connected' Presence: The Emergence of a New Repertoire for Managing Social Relationships in a Changing Communication Technoscape." *Environment and Planning D: Society and Space* 22, no. 1: 135–56.

Ling, Rich. 2008. *New Tech, New Ties*. Cambridge: MIT Press.

Ling, Rich, and Jonathan Donner. 2009. *Mobile Communication*. Oxford: Polity Press.

Lofton, Kathryn. 2017. *Consuming Religion*. Chicago: University of Chicago Press.

Lynch, Gordon. 2012. *The Sacred in the Modern World: A Cultural Sociological Approach*. Oxford: Oxford University Press.

Lyon, David. 2014. "Surveillance and the Eye of God." *Studies in Christian Ethics* 27, no. 1: 21–32.

Malabou, Catherine. (2007) 2012. *The New Wounded: From Neurosis to Brain Damage*. Translated by Steven Miller. New York: Fordham University Press.

Mann, Sandi. 2016. *The Upside of Downtime: Why Boredom is Good*. London: Robinson.

Marino, Gordon. 2015. "The Long Conversation." *New York Times – Opinionator*, 2 June. https://opinionator.blogs.nytimes.com/author/gordon-marino.

Martin, Craig. 2014. *Capitalizing Religion: Ideology and the Opiate of the Bourgeoisie*. New York: Bloomsbury.

McCaffery, Steve. 2012. *The Darkness of the Present: Poetics, Anachronism, and the Anomaly*. Tuscaloosa: The University of Alabama Press.

Miller, Adam S. 2016. *The Gospel According to David Foster Wallace: Boredom and Addiction in an Age of Distraction*. New York: Bloomsbury.

Mitchell, Liam. 2013. "'Because None of Us Are as Cruel as All of Us': Anonymity and Subjectivation." *Ctheory*. Accessed 28 November 2014. http://ctheory.net/articles.aspx?id=720.

– 2014. "Life on Automatic: Facebook's Archival Subject." *First Monday* 19, no. 2 (3 February). https://doi.org/10.5210/fm.v19i2.4825.

Mitchell, W.J.T. 2015. *Image Science: Iconology, Visual Culture, and Media Aesthetics*. Chicago: University of Chicago Press.

Morris, Robert. 1993. "Writing with Davidson: Some Afterthoughts after Doing 'Blind Time IV: Drawing with Davidson.'" *Critical Inquiry* 19, no. 4: 617–27.

Mosurinjohn, Sharday. 2014. "Unraveling the Identity of the Line in Culture: Dominant Lines in the Temporal-Affective Structure of Late Modernity." *International Journal on the Image* 4, no. 4: 113–25.

– 2018. *For Boredom: Conceptual Art and Writing on Boredom as a Crisis of Meaning*. Accessed 29 July 2018. http://forboredom.realtimecollective.com/about-the-project/#.

– 2021. "N. Katherine Hayles." *Political Theology Network*, 9 March. https://politicaltheology.com/n-katherine-hayles.

Mosurinjohn, Sharday, and Nelly Matorina. 2019–20. "For Boredom: A Conceptual Network of Cultural Objects." *Capacious Journal for Emerging Affect Inquiry* 2, nos. 1–2: 174–85.

Mosurinjohn, Sharday, and Galen Watts. 2021. "Religious Studies and the Spiritual Turn." *Method and Theory in the Study of Religion* 33: 1–23. https://doi.org/10.1163/15700682-12341513.

Mulqueen, Maggie. 2019. "Texting Really Is Ruining Personal Relationships." NBC *Think*. https://www.nbcnews.com/think/opinion/texting-really-ruining-personal-relationships-ncna1097461.

Nagel, Thomas. 1974. "What Is It Like to Be a Bat?" *Philosophical Review* 83, no. 4: 435–50.

Nasaw, Jack. 1993. *Going Out: The Rise and Fall of Public Amusements*. New York: Basic Books.

Ngai, Sianne. 2005. *Ugly Feelings*. Cambridge: Harvard University Press.

Ogburn, William F. 1922. *Social Change*. New York: B.W. Huebsch.

O'Neill, Bruce. 2017. *The Space of Boredom: Homelessness in the Slowing Global Order*. Durham: Duke University Press.

Orlowski, Jeff, dir. 2020. *The Social Dilemma*. https://www.thesocial dilemma.com.

Pease, Allison. 2012. *Modernism, Feminism, and the Culture of Boredom*. Cambridge: Cambridge University Press.

Pepperell, Robert. 2009. "An Information Sublime." *Leonardo* 42, no. 5: 384.

Perloff, Marjorie. 2010. *Unoriginal Genius: Poetry by Other Means in the New Century*. Chicago: University of Chicago Press.

Phillips, Adam. 1996. *Monogamy*. New York: Vintage Books.

Pirsig, Robert M. 1974. "The Motorcycle Is Yourself." Radio interview with Tim Wilson. *Ideas*, 2 December. https://www.cbc.ca/news/entertainment/a-fresh-look-at-robert-pirsig-s-zen-and-the-art-of-motorcycle-maintenance-1.2856138.

Priest, Eldritch. 2013. *Boring Formless Nonsense: Experimental Music and the Aesthetics of Failure*. New York: Bloomsbury.

Raczka, Rachel. 2014. "Text Anxiety Is Ruining Our Lives." *Boston.com*. http://www.boston.com/life/2014/09/05/text-anxiety-ruining-our-lives/fO767PCVHJSWiJSk1aAIZN/story.html.

Rancière, Jacques. 2005. *The Politics of Aesthetics: The Distribution of the Sensible*. Translated by Gabriel Rockhill. New York: Bloomsbury.

Raposa, Michael L. 1999. *Boredom and the Religious Imagination*. Charlottesville: University Press of Virginia.

Rizov, Vadim. 2011. "What Just Happened: David Foster Wallace's *The Pale King*." *Slant Magazine*, 1 November. https://www.slantmagazine.com/books/what-just-happened-the-pale-king.

Roubaud, Jacques. 1998. "Introduction: The Oulipo and Combinatorial Art." In *Oulipo Compendium*, edited by Harry Matthews and Alastair Brotchie, 37–44. London: Atlas.

Salecl, Renata. 2006. "Who Am I for Myself? Anxiety and the Tyranny of Choice." Slought Foundation. Accessed 20 August 2013. http://slought.org/content/11318.

– 2009. "Society of Choice." *differences: A Journal of Feminist Cultural Studies* 20, no. 1: 157–80.
– 2011. *The Tyranny of Choice*. London: Profile Books.
Saler, Michael T. 2006. "Modernity and Disenchantment: A Historiographic Review." *American Historical Review* 111, no. 3: 692–716.
– 2012. *As If: Modern Enchantment and the Literary Prehistory of Virtual Reality*. New York: Oxford University Press.
– 2013. "Rethinking Secularism: Modernity, Enchantment, and Fictionalism." *The Immanent Frame: Secularism, Religion and The Public Sphere (an SSRC Blog)*, 20 December. http://blogs.ssrc.org/tif/2013/12/20/modernity-enchantment-and-fictionalism.
Sanghani, Radhika. 2013. "Top Reasons for Trolling Include Boredom and Amusement." *Telegraph*, 27 June. https://www.telegraph.co.uk/technology/news/10145636/Top-reasons-for-trolling-include-boredom-and-amusement.html.
Schaefer, Donovan. 2015. *Religious Affects: Animality, Evolution, and Power.* Durham: Duke University Press.
– 2016. "An Interview with Donovan Schaefer on *Religious Affects*." Interviewed by Christian Von Scheve. *Affective Societies Blog*, 28 November. http://affective-societies.de/en/2016/interviews-portraits/an-interview-with-donovan-schaefer-on-religious-affects.
– 2018. "Beautiful Facts: Science, Secularism, and Affect." In *Feeling Religion*, edited by John Corrigan, 69–92. Durham: Duke University Press.
Schalk, Sami. 2018. *Bodyminds Reimagined: (Dis)ability, Race, and Gender in Black Women's Speculative Fiction*. Durham: Duke University Press.
Schechner, Richard. 1974. "From Ritual to Theatre and Back: The Structure/Process of the Efficacy-Entertainment Dyad." *Educational Theatre Journal* 26, no. 4: 455–81.
Schopenhauer, Arthur. (1818) 1969. *The World as Will and Representation*. Translated by E.J.F. Payne. Vols. 1 and 2. New York: Dover.
Schwartz, Barry. 2004. *The Paradox of Choice: Why More Is Less*. New York: Harper Collins.
Schwartz, Mattathias. 2008. "Malwebolence: The World of Web Trolling." *New York Times Magazine*, 3 August. http://www.nytimes.com/2008/08/03/magazine/03trolls-t.html.
Seigworth, Gregory J., and Melissa Gregg. 2010. "An Inventory of Shimmers." In *The Affect Theory Reader*, edited by Melissa Gregg and Gregory J. Seigworth, 1–25. Durham: Duke University Press.

Sharma, Sarah. 2014. *In the Meantime: Temporality and Cultural Politics*. Durham: Duke University Press.

Shaviro, Steven. 2015. *No Speed Limit: Three Essays on Accelerationism*. Minneapolis: University of Minnesota Press.

Sheehan, Michael. 2011. "Boredom as Religious Experience: David Foster Wallace's *The Pale King*." *Rumpus*, 13 April. http://therumpus.net/2011/04/boredom-as-religious-experience-david-foster-wallace%E2%80%99s-the-pale-king.

Siegel, Eli. 1968. *Hail, American Development*. New York: Definition Press.

Sikoryak, Robert. 2017. *Terms and Conditions: The Graphic Novel*. Parts A and B. Montreal: Drawn & Quarterly.

Slaby, Jan. 2010. "The Other Side of Existence: Heidegger on Boredom." In *Habitus in Habitat II: Other Sides of Cognition*, edited by Sabine Flach and Jan Söffner, 101–20. Bern: Peter Lang.

Smith, Jonathan Z. 1998. "Religion, Religions, Religious." In *Critical Terms for Religious Studies*, edited by Mark C. Taylor, 269–84. Chicago: University of Chicago Press.

Stalder, Felix. 2013. *Digital Solidarity*. Lüneburg: Mute Publishing and PML Books.

Stephens, Paul. 2015. *The Poetics of Information Overload: From Gertrude Stein to Conceptual Writing*. Minneapolis: University of Minnesota Press.

Stewart, Kathleen. 2007. *Ordinary Affects*. Durham: Duke University Press.

Steyerl, Hito. 2012. "The Spam of the Earth: Withdrawal from Representation." *e-Flux* 32 (February). https://www.e-flux.com/journal/32/68260/the-spam-of-the-earth-withdrawal-from-representation.

Stiles, Kristine, and Peter Selz. 1996. *Theories and Documents of Contemporary Art: A Sourcebook of Artists' Writings*. Vol. 35. Berkeley: University of California Press

Supp-Montgomerie, Jenna. 2015. "Affect and the Study of Religion." *Religion Compass* 9/10 (7 October): 335–45. http://doi.org/10.1111/rec3.12166.

Svendsen, Lars. (1999) 2008. *A Philosophy of Boredom*. Translated by John Irons. London: Reaktion Books.

Taves, Ann. 2009. *Religious Experience Reconsidered: A Building-Block Approach to the Study of Religion and Other Special Things*. Princeton, NJ: Princeton University Press.

– 2010. "Experience as Site of Contested Meaning and Value: The Attributional Dog and Its Special Tail." *Religion* 40, no. 4: 317–23. http://doi.org/10.1016/j.religion.2010.09.012.

Toffler, Alvin. 1970. *Future Shock*. New York: Random House.

Tolstoy, Leo. (1875–77) 2000. *Anna Karenina*. Translated by Constance Garnett. Edited by Leonard J. Kent and Nina Berberova. Toronto: Random House of Canada.

Toohey, Peter. 2011. *Boredom: A Lively History*. New Haven: Yale University Press.

Tucker, Ian. 2013. "Bodies and Surveillance: Simondon, Information and Affect." *Distinktion: Scandinavian Journal of Social Theory* 14, no. 1: 30–41. http://dx.doi.org/10.1080/1600910X.2013.766225.

Turkle, Sherry. 2011. *Alone Together: Why We Expect More from Technology and Less from Each Other*. New York: Basic Books.

Urbanová, Ludmila. 2007. "Some Thoughts on the Phatic Communion and Small Talk in Fictional Dialogues." In *Functional Perspectives on Grammar and Discourse*, edited by Christopher Butler, Raquel Hidalgo Downing, and Julia Lavid, 349–58. Philadelphia: John Benjamins Publishing Company.

Vaz, Paulo, and Fernanda Bruno. 2003. "Types of Self-Surveillance: From Abnormality to Individuals 'At Risk.'" *Surveillance & Society* 1, no. 3: 272–91.

Viger, Chris, Robyn Bluhm, and Sharday Mosurinjohn. 2008. "The Binding Problem: Achilles in the 21st Century." In *The Achilles of Rationalist Psychology*, edited by Thomas Lennon and Robert Stainton, 257–85. Dordrecht: Springer.

Virilio, Paul. (1977) 1986. *Speed and Politics: An Essay on Dromology*. New York: Columbia University Press.

Wallace, David Foster. 1993a. "An Interview with David Foster Wallace." By Larry McCaffery. *Review of Contemporary Fiction* 13, no. 2: 127–50.

– 1993b. "E Unibus Pluram: Television and U.S. Fiction." *Review of Contemporary Fiction* 13, no. 2: 151–94.

– 1997. "David Foster Wallace." Television interview. *The Charlie Rose Show*, 27 March. https://charlierose.com/videos/23311.

– (1996) 2006. *Infinite Jest*. 10th Anniversary Edition. New York: Back Bay Books.

– 2007. *A Supposedly Fun Thing I'll Never Do Again: Essays and Arguments*. New York: Little, Brown and Company.

– (2005) 2009. *This is Water: Some Thoughts, Delivered on a Significant Occasion, about Living a Compassionate Life*. New York: Little, Brown and Co.

– 2011. *The Pale King*. New York: Little, Brown and Co.

– n.d. "9/10 Ch. 4 Class Notes." Unpublished handwritten notes, David Foster Wallace Papers Collection, University of Texas at Austin.

Wasserman, Sherri. 2011. "Beyond Information: Ritual, Relationship, and Re-encounter through Mobile Connectivity." *Curator: The Museum Journal* 54, no. 1: 11–24.

Weber, Max. (1917) 1946. "Science as a Vocation." In *From Max Weber: Essays in Sociology*, edited by H.H. Gerth and C. Wright Mills, 129–56. New York: Oxford University Press.

Weiner, Joshua. 2014. "First Reading of Sophia Le Fraga's 'W8ING 4' (1)." *Jacket2*. http://jacket2.org/commentary/first-reading-sophia-le-fragas-w8ing-4.

Whitehead, Nadia. 2014. "People Would Rather Be Electrically Shocked than Left Alone with Their Thoughts." *American Association for the Advancement of Science*, 3 July. https://www.science.org/content/article/people-would-rather-be-electrically-shocked-left-alone-their-thoughts.

Wilson, Jeff. 2014. *Mindful America: The Mutual Transformation of Buddhist Meditation and American Culture*. Oxford: Oxford University Press.

Wilson, Timothy D., David A. Reinhard, Erin C. Westgate, Daniel T. Gilbert, Nicole Ellerbeck, Cheryl Hahn, Casey L. Brown, and Adi Shaked. 2014. "Just Think: The Challenges of the Disengaged Mind." *Science* 345, no. 6192: 75–7.

Woltersdorff, Volker. 2012. "Masochistic Self-shattering between Destructiveness and Productivity." In *Destruction in the Performative*, edited by Alice Lagaay and Michael Lorber, 133–51. Critical Studies 36. Leiden: Brill.

Wuthnow, Robert. 1998. *After Heaven: Spirituality in America since the 1950s*. Los Angeles: University of California Press.

Young, Nora. 2014. "Rediscovering the Reflective Side of Email." *Spark*. http://www.cbc.ca/spark/blog/2014/11/09/rediscovering-the-reflective-side-of-email.

Index

Page numbers in italics indicate illustrations.